RELATIVITY

Relativity

FROM EINSTEIN
TO BLACK HOLES
BY GERALD E. TAUBER

Franklin Watts/1988
New York/London/Toronto/Sydney
A Venture Book

Library of Congress Cataloging-in-Publication Data

Tauber, Gerald E.
Relativity : from Einstein to black holes / by Gerald E. Tauber.
   p. cm.—(A Venture book)
Includes index.
Summary: Surveys Einstein's work on developing his theory of
relativity and discusses recent developments in radioastronomy,
cosmology, and field theory based on Einstein's discovery.
ISBN 0-531-10482-6
1. Relativity (Physics)—Juvenile literature.   2. Einstein,
Albert, 1879–1955—Juvenile literature.   3. Physicists—Biog-
raphy —Juvenile literature.   4. Einstein, Albert, 1879–1955.
[1. Relativity (Physics)   2. Physicists.]   I. Title.
QC173.575.T38 1988
530.1'1—dc19   87-25964   CIP   AC

In Memory of
H. W. and
Ester Rudoler

Quotations from the writings of Albert Einstein that appear on pages 13, 78, 97, and 104 are reprinted with the permission of The Hebrew University of Jerusalem, Israel.

Diagrams by Vantage Art, Inc.

Photographs courtesy of:
Magnum: p. 10 (Philippe Halsman);
Eidgenossische Technische Hochscule: p. 20;
U.S. Air Force: p. 54;
Mrs. Alan Windsor Richards: p. 99;
The Washington Post Co. (c) 1955 and Herblock: p. 115.

CONTENTS

RELATIVITY

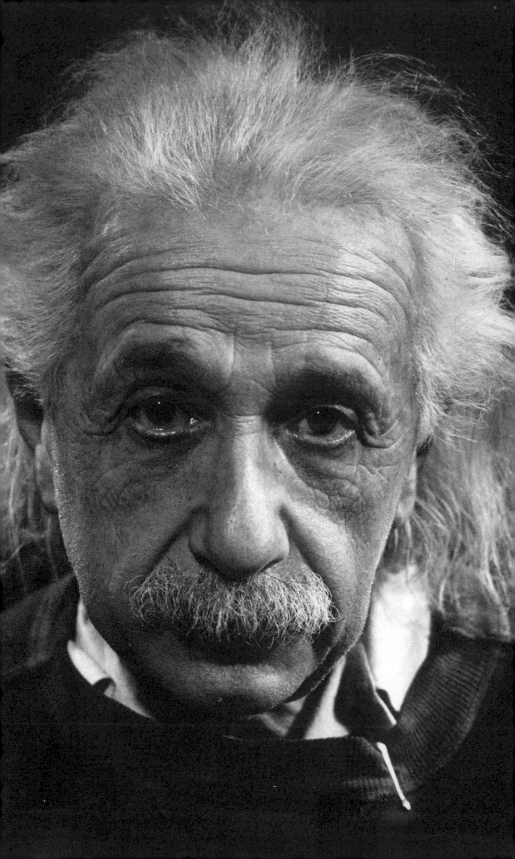

INTRODUCTION
THE GREATNESS
OF EINSTEIN

If you were shown a list of famous scientists you would probably recognize immediately the name Albert Einstein. You even might know that Einstein was a physicist and mathematician. He was actually a theoretical physicist, which means that he did not work in a laboratory, carrying out experiments, but worked with paper and pencil, doing calculations on whatever piece of paper was handy, even the backs of old envelopes.

However, if you were to ask, not many people would be able to tell you exactly what made him so famous, and even fewer could say what his theory of relativity is all about. Some may know that it had to do with rulers and clocks; others will tell you that Einstein explained *gravitation,* the force of attraction between matter. Still others may have heard about the bending of light by the sun or about *space,* which is not flat. Years ago, there was even a popular story that only twelve scientists in the world understood the general theory of relativity. When Einstein first proposed his theory, this may well have been no great exaggeration. Nowadays the theory of relativity is taught in most universities and colleges, and every student of physics has learned it. Although using it does require mastery of some complicated mathematics, the main ideas behind it are quite simple, as you will see later in this book.

Einstein is justifiably considered to be the greatest physicist of our age. But why? There were Marie and Pierre Curie, who (with Antoine Becquerel) discovered radium; Max Planck, who first proposed the existence of the *quantum,* a discrete quantity of energy; and Niels Bohr, who explained the structure of the atom, the smallest particle of a chemical substance—to mention only a few of the geniuses of twentieth-century physics. For their work in that field, all won the Nobel Prize, which is awarded annually for important discoveries; all made significant contributions to our understanding of the physical world. Without detracting from the merits and achievements of these and other great scientists, we can say that there was something in Einstein's mental makeup that distinguished him as a thinker without equal. What was so astonishing in his manner of thinking was that he could discover the underlying principle of a physical situation and penetrate straight to the core of a problem, undeceived by details. To write down mathematical equations in physics is not a particularly difficult task. But Einstein had an uncanny ability to "read" such equations. He could put his finger on any equation (or any part of one) and say "this is the crux of the matter"—and in every single instance it *was* the crux of the matter.

Albert Einstein was not only the greatest physicist of the twentieth century, he was also a great mind and a philosopher. A wonderfully gentle and humble person, Einstein earned well-founded and -deserved world fame, but it meant nothing to him. He was completely without pomposity and pretense. Because social status meant nothing to him, he talked to royalty and common people in the same straightforward and appreciative manner. And he was not indifferent to the needs of others. He took the time and effort to help his fellow human beings and spoke out openly for his beliefs and principles:

> *Concern for man himself and his fate must always form the chief interest of all technical endeavours. Never forget this in the midst of your diagrams and equations.*
>
> Ideas and Opinions

Not merely a scientist dwelling in an "ivory tower," Einstein was a great man who took his obligations to society seriously and lived up to his high standards and principles. He was an example of a person we would like to emulate but have to be satisfied to admire.

EINSTEIN **1**
HIGH SCHOOL
DROPOUT

Albert Einstein was born March 14, 1879, in the little town of Ulm, in southern Germany, near the source of Europe's longest river, the Danube. His parents, Hermann and Pauline, were Jewish. His father, who owned a small electrical business, was a kind of dreamer with a passionate interest in electrical inventions. However, he was unsuccessful in business, and soon after Albert's birth the family, hoping to improve their financial situation, moved to Munich—the city that was later to become the cradle of Nazism.

As a child, Einstein was rather shy and loved to play by himself or take walks in nearby fields and woods. He made his first contact with science at the age of four or five, when his father bought him a small magnetic compass to amuse him while he was sick in bed. He spun the magnetic needle around and around. Here was an object that seemed to have a life and will of its own, always pointing in one direction no matter how it was placed. It was a mystery. As Einstein himself later recalled, "The experience made a deep and lasting impression on me."

In his later quests for understanding he found an able and willing instructor in his Uncle Jakob, who introduced him to mathematics: "When the animal we are hunting cannot be caught, we call it for the time being 'x' and continue to hunt it until it is caught," his uncle said.

School, on the other hand, was unpleasant. He had only disgust for the military discipline that then reigned in most German schools. His teachers impressed him as war-like robots who would have made excellent sergeants but were poor instructors. They, on the other hand, regarded the boy who could not cope with their memory work and discipline as somewhat stupid. One of his exasperated teachers once made a forecast. "You know, Einstein," he said, "you will never amount to anything."

At home, his parents' financial fortunes had gone from bad to worse. The elder Einstein, who always had an open hand for anyone who asked for help, now had to appeal for assistance himself. Cousins in the northern Italian city of Milan offered help, and so the family—with the exception of Albert, who still had three years before finishing high school—left to seek their fortune in Milan. Now, suddenly, at the age of fifteen, Albert was alone and lonely. Although he would need the graduation diploma to enter a German university, he decided to leave school and join his family in Italy. He managed to obtain from the family doctor a medical certificate saying that he needed rest in a sunny climate. However, even before he could present the certificate to the principal he was expelled from school "on the grounds that his presence in the class is disruptive and affects the other students." Albert Einstein had become a dropout.

Federal Institute of Technology

In Italy he felt free for the first time. With nobody to guide every step of his daily routine, he roamed through the countryside. He visited museums and art galleries, attended concerts and lectures, and read books and more books. His thirst for knowledge was unquenchable. But the idyll could not last. The electrical engineering business his father had started so enthusiastically had encountered one setback after another, and the young searcher was told to forget his "philosophical nonsense" and settle down to a "practical" life of self-support.

Albert could not picture for himself a career burdened with an office routine, nor could he accept his father's profession, that of an electrochemical engineer. His only desire was to lead an intellectual life with leisure to solve the mysterious puzzles of nature. He decided he needed a university education. Since he had not graduated from high school, he could not enter any university in Germany. However, in Zurich, in the German-speaking part of Switzerland, there was the country's famous Federal Institute of Technology (ETH), similar to Massachusetts Institute of Technology (MIT) in the United States. To be admitted, it was only necessary to pass an entrance examination, and, despite his youth (Einstein was only sixteen at the time), he was permitted to take the examination. He failed it, not in mathematics and physics, as is often said— in those subjects he excelled—but in botany and in the languages. Einstein later admitted that the failure was entirely his fault, since he lacked formal education in these subjects. He was advised to complete his secondary education at the high school in Aarau, a little town at the border of Germany and Switzerland. There, among pleasant surroundings and friends, Einstein finished his studies. (Professor Winteler, at whose home he stayed, became his close friend and advisor, and his son later married Einstein's sister Maya.) Einstein obtained the diploma that opened the doors of ETH. The former dropout had become a university student.

Einstein threw himself enthusiastically into his studies, but even the famous teachers of the institute were not sufficient for him. Often he cut classes, spending his time in the library studying the works of Heinrich Hertz, the discoverer of radio waves; Hermann von Helmholtz, a proponent of the theory of sound and light; and many others. Fortunately, his friend Marcel Grossmann kept an excellent set of lecture notes that Einstein frequently copied when he had cut classes and examinations were near.

At the age of twenty-one Einstein graduated from ETH. Now he had to stand on his own feet and try to make a living. He loved to teach, and several of his professors had indicated that an assistant lecturer's position would be available to him after graduation. However, when he later approached his former professors about such a position, he met only with refusals. Whether they were jealous of the brilliant student, resented his forthright and independent manner, or whether his religious and national background influenced their decision (Einstein was Jewish and a German, at least by birth), the fact remains that he did not obtain the coveted instructorship. For the next few years he taught in a technical high school, and he was later a tutor in a private school. There he and his charges became very close friends, but when he asked for a larger share of their education, he lost his job. So, Albert Einstein, the former dropout who managed to graduate from a university, was now unemployed.

Patent Examiner

Marcel Grossmann, whose lecture notes had been so helpful to Einstein and who was later to become a collaborator, heard of his friend's plight. He spoke to his father, who recommended Einstein to his friend Friedrich Haller, director of the Swiss Patent Office in Berne, the capital of

Switzerland. The director took a liking to the shy young man, whose wide knowledge of scientific questions he recognized immediately. So, finally, Einstein got a position as patent examiner. His task consisted of examining applications for patents to see whether the particular inventions contained something new for which patents should be granted. His ability to recognize the essential feature of any problem made him well suited for his job. It left him ample time to perform his own calculations, which he used to hide furtively in his desk whenever he heard someone approaching. It was, as he called it, a "shoemaker's job." He later advised young students to get similar shoemaker jobs, in which they were not paid for doing research but for something else and could still do their own work.

In one year, 1905, Einstein published four research papers, any one of which would have made him a name in scientific circles. The first one, on the so-called *Brownian motion* (named after the Scottish botanist Robert Brown [1773–1858] who, using a highly magnifying microscope, first observed the phenomenon), dealt with a peculiar motion of pollen particles suspended in a fluid. These particles—barely visible even under the microscope—dart in all directions as if they were alive, the motion becoming livelier the higher the temperature of the fluid. If we trace the path of such a particle, we find a highly irregular zigzag line that apparently follows no inner law, as if it were just a random motion (fig. 1). Einstein showed that these jerky motions are caused by the many pushes the suspended particle receives from the still smaller molecules of the fluid (which cannot be seen even under the microscope) that collide with it. It is as if a punching bag were suspended from the ceiling and people were trying their skill on it from all sides. Since, on the whole, the blows on opposite sides will more or less balance, we might expect the particle to remain more or less at rest. But if we

*Einstein's position at the Swiss Patent Office in Berne
left him ample time to pursue his own research.*

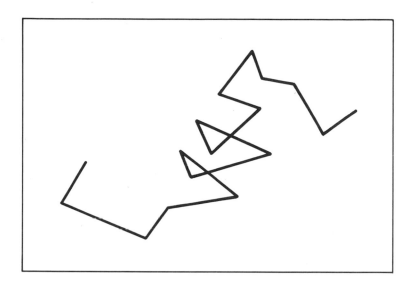

Figure 1.

do we are forgetting the laws of probability. Einstein showed that statistical fluctuations—analogous to runs of luck when throwing dice—would cause imbalances large enough to give the particle an erratic, zigzag motion that can be observed under a microscope. If one waited long enough, the random zigzags would give rise to varying amounts of movement, which could be calculated by statistical methods. That such an apparently random motion should actually satisfy a very definite mathematical law that can be verified by direct observation was highly surprising. It demonstrated Einstein's uncanny ability to apply statistical reasoning and gave strong support to the atomic theory of matter, which assumes matter to be made of molecules and atoms.

If you have ever gone through a door that opened automatically when you approached it or have been in an elevator whose door closed only when someone entered it, chances are that it was operated by a *photoelectric cell.* When light hits certain metals, electrons—negatively charged particles—are emitted from the metal. These electrons in turn generate an electric current that operates the mechanism that closes or opens the door. This phenomenon is called the photoelectric effect (fig. 2a, b), the subject of Einstein's second research paper in 1905. It has been found that the number of electrons, and thus the electric current, increases in the same way as does the amount of light falling on the metal. For example, if we double the intensity, i.e., power of the light source, the electric current is doubled. However, the energy of the emitted electrons does not increase if the intensity is increased. Moreover, the energy of the electrons depends on the color of the light; for some colors, no electrons are emitted, no matter how intense the light.

A few years earlier, in 1900, Max Planck had deduced his famous "radiation formula" by assuming that somehow energy is emitted not continuously but in small packages called *quanta* (plural of the Latin word *quantum,* meaning "how much"). Einstein now showed that under certain circumstances light also behaves like particles; nowadays these "light particles" are called *photons.* The photoelectric effect then arises from a bombardment of certain metals by photons, resulting in the emission of electrons.

Einstein's third research paper was concerned with the nature of molecules. We all know that if we drop a lump of sugar into water it dissolves and diffuses through the water, making the liquid somewhat more sticky. Thinking of water as a structureless fluid and the sugar molecules as small hard spheres, Einstein was able to find not only the size of the sugar molecules but a value for "Avogadro's number," the number of molecules in a gas

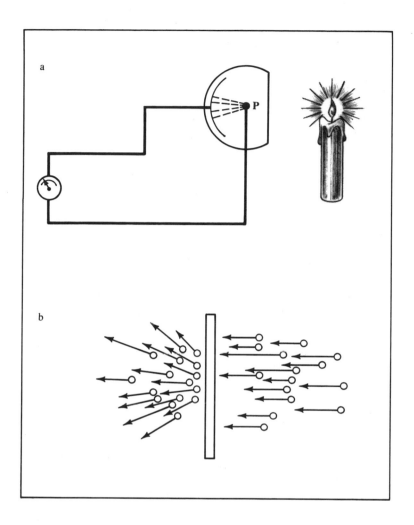

*Figure 2a. When light falls on the photo-sensitive plate (**P**), electrons (broken lines) are emitted, closing the electric circuit. Figure 2b. According to Einstein, photons (right) bombard the plate. If their energy (or frequency) is greater than (or equal to) a certain value, electrons (left) are emitted.*

in a certain standard volume under specified conditions. True, this quantity had already appeared earlier in the theory of gases, but not until then in connection with solutions in liquids. Einstein submitted his paper on the nature of molecules as his doctoral thesis to the University of Zurich. It was rejected as being too short. He added one sentence—and it was accepted.

The paper—which made Einstein famous, of course—was on what is now known as the *special theory of relativity*. It will be the subject of a future chapter, but first we have to examine some basic concepts.

To measure a physical quantity means to associate it with a definite number expressed in a suitable unit. For example, if we want to measure the mass of a body we first choose a suitable unit, say, a "gram" or an "ounce." Then we place the unknown mass in one pan of a scale and balance it with the required number of grams or ounces. The number of grams or ounces then gives us the mass of the body (what we really measure is the weight of the body, which is numerically equal to its mass). Similarly, if we wish to measure the distance between two points, we use a ruler or measuring tape. The number of times we have to place it, starting from the first point until we reach the second, gives us the distance in feet or meters. To measure the time interval between two events, such as the beginning and end of a race, we use a clock—preferably a stopwatch. When the divisions on the face of the clock are marked in seconds, the number of divisions the hand of the clock has traveled will give us the time that has elapsed in seconds.

Frames of Reference

In order to specify the location of a particular position, we need a "reference system" to which positions and motions

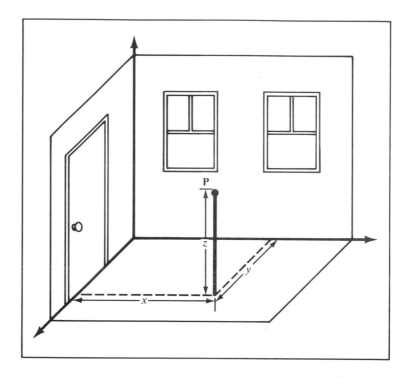

Figure 3.

can be referred. For example, if you live on the sixteenth
floor of an apartment house on the southwest corner of
Ninth Street and Fifth Avenue in New York City, your
position is exactly specified. The intersection of Ninth Street
and Fifth Avenue locates a particular apartment house, while
the sixteenth floor gives the height above the street level.
There are many more examples of such *frames of reference*. You could use two adjacent walls and the floor of
your room to fix the position of the top of a pole. The
position of the top of the pole P is fixed by giving its
height *(z)* and distance from the two walls *(x, y)*. The three
numbers *x, y, z* form a *Cartesian coordinate system* (fig.
3). With the help of such a coordinate system we can

locate any position in space. We simply choose a convenient reference point and three axes mutually perpendicular to each other (like the walls and floor in your room). The three numbers x, y, and z, giving the distances (in convenient units) along the three axes, are the coordinates of the required location.

There exists an endless number of such systems, each with different points of reference or orientations of axes or both. We may ask whether among the large variety of such frames of reference there is a "privileged," or special, one—say, centered at the Earth—to which all measurements should be referred. Indeed, until the Middle Ages, the Earth was accepted as the natural center of the universe to which all positions (and motions) were referred. Later, the sun became the "natural" center since all the planets (including the Earth) revolve around it. Today we know that the sun is just one of millions of stars—and not a particularly large and bright one at that—in the Milky Way, which, in turn, is just one of many, many galaxies in the universe. There is no particular center to the universe. We can choose any convenient coordinate system, whether it be the walls of a room, the streets in a city, or Earth itself—just so long as we understand that the choice has been one of convenience and not necessity.

Relative Motion

Not only the position but also the motion of an object has to be related to a frame of reference. If we say the speed of car A is 50 miles (80 km) per hour, we mean this is the speed relative to, say, a hitchhiker standing on the road (fig. 4). Car A will appear to be moving at only 20 miles (32 km) per hour to a passenger in car B, which is itself traveling at 30 miles (48 km) per hour in the same direction. An observer on Mars (assuming that one were there)

Figure 4.

will think differently. For him not only is the car in motion, but also Earth turns around its axis and revolves around the sun. But even Mars and the sun and all the other planets are moving, and the motion of the car will be vastly different when viewed from one of the fixed stars. (Of course, the motion of the car itself will be insignificant compared with that of our planet Earth.) So, motion is really *relative* and depends on the position—in space and time—of the particular observer.

Anyone who flies in an airplane or rides in a train, for example, almost instinctively adopts the plane or train as his or her frame of reference, provided the flight or ride is along a straight path and at constant speed. A person may even walk along the aisle without being aware that the train or airplane is moving. It is only when the train gains (or loses) speed or the plane takes off (or lands) that the person will be aware of being in motion. Undoubtedly, when you have traveled by train or bus you have noticed that the train or bus seemed to be standing still and the landscape and telephone poles seemed to be moving in the opposite direction. Of course, you knew that this was not so. Suppose the train or bus had no windows; then you could never tell whether the train or bus was moving or not. Long ago, the Roman poet Virgil put it clearly: "Leaving the port, the land and cities are receding." Obviously, there is something special about motion in a straight line at constant speed and, consequently, about reference systems moving in such a fashion. In his first law of motion, Newton stated, "Every body at rest stays at rest and every body in motion stays in motion in a straight line, unless acted upon by an external force." In other words, if there are no external forces, there is no acceleration, or change of velocity. Observers moving relative to each other at a constant speed (fig. 4), such as those in cars A and B (as well as the hitchhiker), are in a somewhat special position. Each one could claim to be at rest and that the others are moving, relatively, with constant speed forward or backward, as the case may be. Such observers are called *inertial observers,* and the corresponding frames of reference are called *inertial frames of reference.*

Principle of Relativity

Let us go one step further. Suppose a bird is flying over or along the road that cars A and B are traveling. If passengers in the two cars were to measure the speed of the bird at any time, they would obtain different values, since each would refer the motion to his or her own (inertial) frame of reference. However, they would agree on the change of velocity (change of speed as well as direction of flight). These quantities are the difference of the velocities at subsequent times and independent of the particular inertial frame of reference. Since the laws of mechanics are concerned with changes in motion, we arrive at the result that, as far as the laws of mechanics are concerned, *all* inertial observers are equivalent. To put it briefly: *If the laws of mechanics are valid in one inertial frame of reference, then they are valid in any other inertial frame of reference.* This, in a restricted sense, is known as the principle of relativity—restricted, because it deals only with inertial frames of reference; that is, coordinate systems moving relative to each other with uniform motion (constant speed and in a straight line). This principle of relativity was nothing new in physics; it had been known to Galileo and Newton, but they also talked about absolute rest and absolute uniform motion relative to a featureless absolute space. Einstein extended this principle by making it a *universal* one, including *all* phenomena, not only mechanical ones. In doing so he also abolished the notions of absolute rest and absolute uniform motion. This is one of the two pillars on which the special theory of relativity stands; the second one deals with the speed of light, which we shall consider in the next chapter.

THE **3** ETHER

In 1862 the English physicist James Clerk Maxwell predicted the existence of *electromagnetic waves*. He also showed that the speed at which such waves travel is exactly the speed of light, namely 186,000 miles (300,000 km) per second. This immediately suggested not only that light is a wave but that in particular it is an electromagnetic wave. A few years later, in 1887, Heinrich Hertz was able to produce electromagnetic waves with frequencies of about a million to a hundred million hertz. (A hertz [Hz] is the unit used to measure frequencies of electromagnetic waves and corresponds to one oscillation per second.) Hertz was not only able to produce electromagnetic waves, but he also showed that they could be reflected by metallic surfaces and exhibited other properties possessed by light. In short, the behavior of electromagnetic waves was so similar to that of light as to leave little doubt that light itself is just a form of electromagnetic waves, the only difference being the size of the frequency.

Now, if light was a wave motion—say, like sound—it was believed that there had to be a medium, a substance through which the waves travel. Take, for example, a bell and place it in a glass jar. You will see it and hear the sound it makes. Now connect the jar to a pump and remove the air. The sound will get weaker and weaker until it stops completely, but the bell can still be seen. The air is the medium for the sound waves, and without it there are no waves and no sound. The fact that we can see the bell, even though there is no air in the jar, means that light waves can travel *in vacuo*, in empty space. But then, what is the medium, the "substance," that carries the light waves? To deal with this question, people "invented" one, a hypothetical medium they called *ether* (meaning "upper air," which the Greeks thought permeated all of space). It is not to be confused with the chemical substance used to anesthetize patients before operations.

This ether was imagined to have some very peculiar properties: it was supposed to fill all space, it was weightless, it could not be seen or felt, and it was perfectly elastic but also at the same time perfectly rigid (in order to support the light properly). However, its most peculiar property was the motion of a body, such as Earth, with respect to it.

Motion Relative
to the Ether

The ether—if it existed—would not only be the medium through which electromagnetic waves—and hence light—are propagated, but it would also play the role of an absolute frame of reference with respect to which motion should be observed. As long as we were talking about accelerations and changes of velocity, all inertial frames were equivalent, but if a universal speed—the speed of light in empty space (or rather in the ether)—*did* exist, a vehicle's uniform motion through the ether could be determined.

We can illustrate this by a simple example (fig. 5). Consider a stream of water (of width *s*) moving at a certain speed *(v)* and a boat moving at speed *c* (in still water). If the boat moves downstream a distance *s* and then returns to its starting point, it can be shown that the round

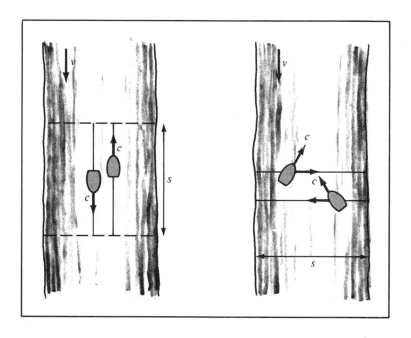

Figure 5. A boat, whose speed (in still water) is c moves in a stream of width s and speed v. Left: It moves downstream a distance s and then upstream, returning to its starting line. Right: It moves across the stream and then back to its original position. (Note that the boat has to be faced into the stream both times). The time taken for the return trip in the second case (right diagram) is less than the time for the return trip in the first case (left diagram).

trip will take *longer* than it would take for the boat to cross the stream and then return to the shore from which it started. This may surprise you, but remember that in the first case the trip upstream will more than offset the gain of the downstream motion. On the other hand, crossing the stream in either direction will take the same time. Now, let the boat represent rays of light traveling at speed c (c usually denotes the speed of light in empty space; $c = 186,000$ miles [300,000 km] per second), and the stream the motion of Earth. Thus, the apparent speed of light is different along the motion of Earth and at right angles to it. Hence, if we call the frame of reference in which light travels with speed c (in still water, in our example) "the frame of absolute rest," the apparent speed of light will be different in any other frame, for example, greater than c in the direction in which the frame is traveling (along the stream, in our example) relative to the frame at rest, and less than c in the opposite direction (against the stream). Moreover, as in the first case in our example, light travels a certain distance along (and against) Earth's motion. In the second case, it travels the same distance (and back) perpendicular to it. From our illustration we then conclude that the two times should not be equal, the second one being shorter. By measuring the difference in the times (and knowing distance s and speed c), the absolute speed (v) of Earth with respect to the ether could then be found.

Michelson-Morley Experiment

To find this difference in the times light travels along and perpendicular to Earth's motion was the purpose of a series of very careful experiments carried out by Albert A. Michelson and Edward W. Morley in 1887. In their experiment, light from a source is directed to a half-silvered

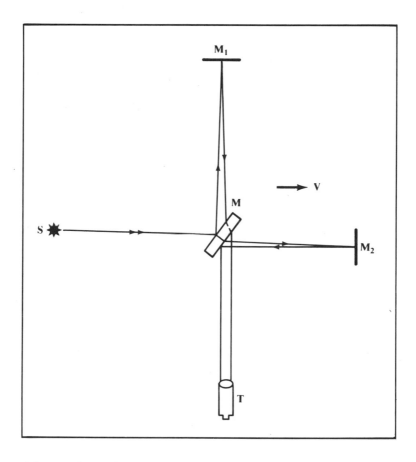

Figure 6. Light from a source (S) is partially reflected and partially transmitted by a half-silvered mirror (M). It continues in two directions at right angles to each other. Each is reflected by a plane mirror (M₁ and M₂) and enters telescope (T). The whole apparatus moves with speed V, the earth's speed relative to the ether.

mirror. Part of the light is transmitted, and part is reflected in two directions perpendicular to each other. After further reflections by two plane mirrors, both rays are collected in a telescope (fig. 6). The apparatus was accurate enough to measure the smallest interference between the light rays along the two paths. Then the whole apparatus was rotated around a vertical axis, and hence the directions of the two arms interchanged. However, no change in the interference pattern was observed. The experiment was repeated in different directions and at different times of Earth's motion around the sun, but the result was always the same. The speed of light was the same whether it was measured along or at right angles to Earth's motion.

Several explanations were put forward. Michelson suggested that perhaps Earth "drags the ether along," and thus the motion of Earth relative to the ether could not be detected. However, this hypothesis had to be discarded when it became evident that the motion of starlight required a "stationary ether." More interesting was the explanation proffered by G. F. FitzGerald and H. A. Lorentz. They suggested that measuring rods seem to shrink along the motion of the Earth (or other objects) with respect to the ether. This contraction, called the *Lorentz-FitzGerald contraction,* would be sufficient to offset the negative result of the Michelson-Morley experiment. The amazing thing is that we are unable to observe that contraction by an experiment save one like that of Michelson and Morley, since everything—including our measuring instruments and the retina of the eye—experiences such a contraction in the direction of the motion. Later we shall see that the Lorentz-FitzGerald contraction is a natural consequence of the special theory of relativity.

The significance of the null result of the Michelson-Morley experiment lies not so much in the fact that relative motion with respect to the ether cannot be detected, but rather in the fact that there is no need for an ether *at all.* You will recall that the ether was believed to play the role of an absolute frame of reference, relative to which (absolute) motion can occur, which should be detectable.

Now, the Michelson-Morley experiment and similar investigations showed that no such motion can be detected, and hence the ether loses its special role as an absolute frame of rest. We can put it differently and say that the principle of relativity holds not only for mechanical phenomena (in which changes of velocities are involved) but also for electric and magnetic phenomena (involving velocities themselves). In other words, *all* inertial frames of reference are equivalent, even those that move with the speed of light.

But what about the need for a medium through which electromagnetic waves are supposed to travel? If there is no ether, then there is no medium to carry the waves. This is essentially true; it has been shown that electric and magnetic disturbances produce electromagnetic *fields,* space through which these forces act. These fields are transmitted with the speed of light and act as the carriers of electromagnetic waves. The situation may be compared—although loosely—to masses of water in an ocean buffeting the shore. The water waves are carried by the water masses in a way that is analogous to the way electromagnetic fields carry electromagnetic waves.

Speed of Light

The result of the Michelson-Morley experiment is rather startling in another respect. When we talked about a car moving at a speed of 50 miles (80 km) per hour, we had to specify, "with respect to a hitchhiker standing on the road" (fig. 4). No such limitation is necessary when we talk about the speed of light. The speed of light in empty space is an *absolute constant* and, incidentally, the maximum speed attainable in nature. Suppose that at a certain time a number of people are in the same place. Some are traveling in cars, others walking in one direction, and others in the opposite direction—all at different speeds. If a flash of light is now sent out from that place, after one second it will be 186,000 miles (or 300,000 km) from *all* persons on that road, even if they are traveling in opposite directions. It will be 186,000 miles from you, who are traveling in one direction, but it will also be 186,000 miles from your friend, who is traveling in the opposite direction. This seems unexplainable unless we assume that our watches and clocks have been affected somehow by the motion. In fact, they have. That is how this disagreement is explained by the special theory of relativity, as we shall see later.

This, then, is the second postulate—the second pillar—on which the special theory of relativity is built: *The speed of light (in empty space) measured by any observer remains the same, namely 186,000 miles (300,000 km) per second.* It does not matter whether the source of light is moving or not; it also does not matter whether the observer, the person receiving the light, is moving or remains still. In other words, the light beam from the headlight (or taillight) of a moving car would always have the same speed, no matter what the motion of the car. This would be true even if the car could move with nearly the speed of light with respect to the road. As long as we assumed the existence of an ether that carries the light wave, the postulate seemed obvious and perhaps even trivial, for no matter how a light wave is started, once it is moving it is carried by the ether at that constant speed with which waves are propagated. But, if you remember, we have found discrepancies—the null effect of the Michelson-Morley experiment—and finally discarded the ether as being "superfluous." Taking this point of view, the constancy of light becomes a real assumption, a postulate.

The two postulates, the principle of relativity and the constancy of the speed of light, seem straightforward enough, but there is an "apparent" inconsistency between them. Apparent, because Einstein was able to reconcile them and formulate his special theory of relativity. Let us illustrate the situation by means of a hypothetical experiment. Suppose you are flying in a superjet traveling at the speed of light. A mirror is in front of you. As seen from the ground, the light leaving your face travels at speed c, the speed of light, independent of the motion of the jet. This is in accordance with the postulate of the constancy of the speed of light. However, as seen from the jet, your image will disappear, since you are moving at exactly the same speed as the light leaving your face, and by the time it would return from the mirror you have passed it. But this is a violation of the principle of relativity, since you now know that you are moving. In other words, we have set up an experiment that can determine absolute motion. On the other hand, if we want to keep the principle of relativity intact, the speed of the light, as seen from the ground, would be $c + c$, the sum of the speed of the jet and the speed of the light itself. This is a violation of the second postulate, the constancy of the light. At this stage a person of lesser stature than Einstein would have given up or tried to modify one of the two postulates. But not Einstein. He recognized the simplicity and correctness of *both* postulates and realized that the solution must lie somewhere else—something must be wrong with our notions about time and space. As a result of an analysis of these concepts it became evident that there is not the least incompatibility between the principle of relativity and the constancy of the speed of light. A logically rigid theory based on *both* of these principles can be established—the special theory of relativity.

It took the boldness of an Einstein to perceive that the two postulates on which the special theory of relativity is based are inconsistent only if we accept Newton's axioms of an absolute space and an absolute time. Ever since Newton, it had been accepted that all frames of reference can be represented by some kind of markers identifying locations in space, but that all observers make use of the *same* universal time. In our previous example of the moving cars, for instance, both inevitably use the same time when making their measurements. Moreover, it has been assumed that the time interval between two events, such as the time that elapsed between car A's passing one milestone and then another or the distance traversed (in that time), is independent of the motion of the observer, the driver of car B. Yet this need not be so. Is it not conceivable that one reference system moving relative to another, even at a constant speed, has its own space and time measurements, which need not coincide with the others? Only if we take it as an unalterable fact that the times measured in the two systems are the *same* are the two postulates indeed self-contradictory. This assumption seems to be so intuitively correct that it has simply been taken for granted.

It is borne out by everyday experience, if—and here is the point—we are dealing with velocities much smaller than the speed of light. In that case the differences in the measurements in the two systems are so small that for practical purposes they can be neglected. However, it must be stressed that these differences do exist, as we shall see.

Simultaneity

Two events (happenings) are said to occur *simultaneously*—that is, at the same time—when they are observed at the same time. Suppose that you are standing exactly midway between places A and B and are equipped with an apparatus (for example, two mirrors inclined at 90 degrees) enabling you to observe both places A and B simultaneously. Now suppose lightning strikes the two places (fig. 7a). If the light flashes from both places reach you at the same time—we assume that it takes light the same time to travel to you from A as it does from B—we say

Figure 7a.

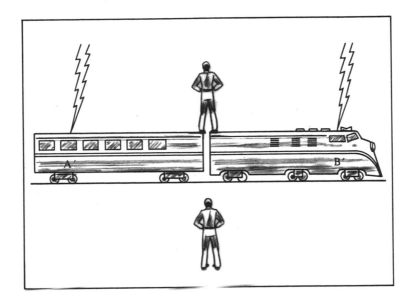

Figure 7b.

that the lightning has struck A and B simultaneously. However, a person traveling in a fast-moving car—and we mean *really* fast-moving—and equipped with a similar apparatus will say that the lightning struck B *before* it struck A. She is rushing toward B (and away from A), and thus the light flash from B will reach her apparatus before the corresponding one from A does.

Now let us consider another example. Suppose there is a very long train traveling at a very high speed and that lightning strikes two points, A′ and B′, near either end of the train. An observer on that train, situated halfway between A′ and B′, will say that the lightning has struck A′ and B′ simultaneously, if the light flashes from these two points reach him at the same time (fig. 7b). (We have assumed that he is also equipped with some kind of apparatus that allows him to observe the flashes from A′ and B′ at the same time.) On the other hand, you are standing on the embankment, also midway between the two points where lightning has struck. Nevertheless, you will say that the lightning struck A' *before* it struck B'. The train is moving away from you, and thus the light beam from A' will reach your apparatus before the corresponding one from B'.

From these two examples we then conclude that any two events (for example, the two strokes of lightning at A and B) that are simultaneous with respect to one system of reference are *not* simultaneous with respect to another system of reference moving relative to the first one. In other words, events that are simultaneous with respect to the embankment (or the road) are not simultaneous with respect to the moving car (or moving train); and, vice versa, events that are simultaneous with respect to the moving car (or moving train) are not simultaneous with respect to the (stationary) observer. This principle is referred to as *relativity of simultaneity*. Every reference system has its *own* particular time; unless we are told which reference system a statement of time refers to, there is no meaning in a statement of the time of an event.

Clocks Appear
to Run Slow

Since our two observers cannot agree on simultaneous events, events happening at the same time, they will certainly not agree on events that occur at different times. Suppose the lightning strikes B five minutes after it strikes A (fig. 7a). The driver of the moving car will say that the lightning struck B a little less than five minutes after it struck A. His watch seems to have slowed down. We can demonstrate this by constructing a special type of clock that consists of a vertical meter stick with a mirror at each end. A pulse of light is reflected between the mirrors, and

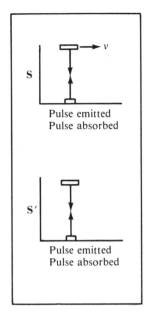

Pulse emitted
Pulse absorbed

Pulse emitted
Pulse absorbed

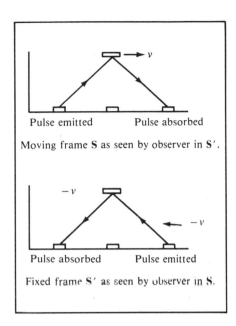

Pulse emitted   Pulse absorbed

Moving frame S as seen by observer in S'.

Pulse absorbed   Pulse emitted

Fixed frame S' as seen by observer in S.

Figure 8a.   *Figure 8b.*

some kind of device is attached to one of the mirrors to give a "tick" each time the pulse of light strikes it (fig. 8a). Since we know the distance between the mirrors and the speed of light, it is simple to calculate the time it takes for light to travel from one mirror to the other and back again, which is the time between consecutive ticks. Two such clocks are constructed. One is kept on the ground, and the second is mounted in a fast-moving airplane or spacecraft. Both the observer on the ground and the pilot will obtain the same readings on *their* particular clocks. However, as seen from the ground, the path of the light in the moving clock—the one in the plane—will describe a zigzag (fig. 8b). It is longer than the path of the stationary clock, because the airplane is moving horizontally. Since the speed of light is the same for both, the time between ticks of the moving clock is longer—the clock has slowed down. Exactly the same argument applies to the pilot of the spacecraft. To him the light pulse of the clock on the ground follows a zigzag path (but in the opposite direction). The clock has slowed down. The effect is mutual. *Every* observer finds that clocks in motion relative to him or her tick more slowly. But our discussion has been based on a rather unusual type of clock. Are the results also correct for conventional clocks that use springs, quartz crystals, or other mechanisms? The answer is yes, because we can always synchronize our mirror clocks with conventional ones on the ground and in an airplane or spacecraft.

Measuring Rods Appear Shortened

Similar considerations apply to the measurement of distances. We measure the length of an object by applying both ends of a foot rule or meter stick to both ends at the *same* time (or, if the object is large, by successive applications of the foot rule). There is no difficulty involved when the object to be measured is at rest relative to us (as most things are). But have you ever tried to measure the length of a very fast-moving train? A person on that supertrain will have no difficulty at all, since he is at rest with respect to the train. Because of the relativity of simultaneity, our results—even if we are lucky enough to obtain them—will differ from his. We will get values that are smaller than his, the amount of difference depending on the speed of the train. In our eyes the moving train seems to have shrunk in the direction of motion. (It should be mentioned, however, that the effect will only be noticeable if the speed of the train is very great, approaching the speed of light. In everyday experience, in which one deals with velocities much smaller than the speed of light, the effect will not be observable.)

Let us now imagine the following experiment. A passenger in a fast-moving car—we are talking again about a futuristic car traveling at a speed nearly that of light—wants to measure the length of a fixed stretch of the road. The ends are marked by two posts. He has a very accurate stopwatch. Now, distance is equal to speed multiplied by time. Since the speed of the car is known (from the speedometer), all he has to do is to notice the time that has elapsed in driving from one post to the other. He starts his stopwatch as he passes the first post and stops it when he passes the second post. However, because of *time dilation*, the slowing down of clocks, the time read by his stopwatch is less than that shown by one placed on the ground. Consequently, the length of the "moving stretch of road" is less than the actual length measured on the ground.

Lorentz Transformations

The results of our previous discussion can now be summarized as follows: Experience has led us to the conviction that, on one hand, the principle of relativity holds true and that, on the other hand, the speed of light (in a vacuum) is an absolute constant (equal to $c = 186,000$ miles [300,000 km] per second) irrespective of the motion of the source or observer. These two apparently self-contradictory hypotheses are reconcilable, provided that each (inertial) observer employs a frame of reference with its own space and time measurements. In his or her particular system of coordinates (characterized by the space coordinates x, y, and z and the time t), the observer is at rest. Furthermore, in his or her own reference system, every observer applies his or her own measuring rods and clocks. Only if they are applied to another system—moving relative to the first—will the results be different.

The question now arises whether it is possible to find a connection between the two systems, a *transformation* that permits us to relate the measurements in one frame of reference to another one moving relative to it at constant velocity. The answer is a definite yes. Einstein showed that the two pillars of relativity are in fact sufficient to obtain a very definite relation between the two sets of quantities. The sets of equations that relate the space and time coordinates of one inertial frame of reference to another inertial frame are known as the *Lorentz transformations*. They do not coincide with the customary equations that were in use for many years. However, if the velocities involved are small compared with the speed of light, the corrections to the usual formulae become exceedingly small and for all practical purposes may be neglected. Thus, the usual laws of mechanics remain valid in ordinary experience, in which one deals with small velocities. On the other hand, if one deals with large velocities, approaching the speed of light, the effect becomes noticeable, as envisaged by the Lorentz-FitzGerald contraction and time dilation, a consequence of the Lorentz transformations.

Four-Dimensional World of Minkowski

A few years later, in 1908, Hermann Minkowski, a former teacher of Einstein at ETH, interpreted the special theory of relativity from a new point of view. He did not change any of its substance but translated Einstein's ideas from the world of physics into the world of geometry. It is interesting to note that at first Einstein was very skeptical of the idea but later found it of great importance, especially when he developed the general theory of relativity.

In order to specify an event, a happening, it is not sufficient to give the space coordinates, but we also need time. Earlier we talked about locating your position. But it is not enough to say that you are on the sixteenth floor of an apartment building at Ninth Street and Fifth Avenue in New York. You have to add the time, say, on April 10, 1987, at such and such an hour, since you might not be there an hour later. So you see, our world really has four dimensions, three for space and one for time. The difference between our usual thinking and Einstein's is that we keep space and time separate, but in relativity they are combined into a four-dimensional coordinate system, as is evidenced by the Lorentz transformations, which involve them on an equal footing.

The idea of representing time in a geometrical manner is not new. We are all familiar with those instruments that record the daily temperature from hour to hour in the shape of a "graph." Here the time is read off along a horizontal line and the corresponding temperature along a vertical one. Sales curves are another example. Time is again marked along the horizontal axis, and the number of items sold, such as automobiles, appears along the vertical axis. In all these cases time appears as a length. More interesting are the so-called "graphic timetables" (fig. 9). On the horizontal axis we plot the distance (in miles or kilometers) between two stations, say, New York and Cleveland; on the vertical axis, the time (in hours). If the train moves at constant speed, we get a straight line. If it stops at certain stations, we get broken lines, because time passes without any motion. The slower the train, the steeper becomes its graph. The angle becomes 90° (that is, the line is vertical) if the train stands still, and nearly 0° (that is, the line is nearly horizontal) if the train moves very

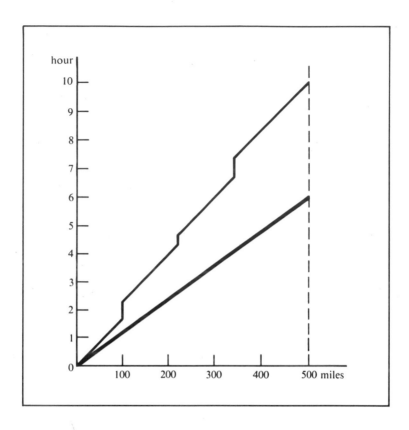

Figure 9. The heavy line indicates an express train which requires six hours to cover 500 miles at constant speed. The thin line represents a slower train which needs ten hours to cover the same distance. Not only is its speed slower, but it makes three stops as shown by the vertical line segments. In both cases the line is the "world line" of the respective train.

fast. In the first case, time passes without any change in distance, while in the second case—even in a short time— the change in distance is very great. Now imagine the horizontal line replaced by the three space dimensions and, presto, you have a four-dimensional world. In practice, one neglects the two extra space dimensions and limits oneself to the simple graphic timetable type of representation. The graph of the moving train is called its *world line*.

Let us now go back to our train. Suppose between New York and Cleveland there are people standing on the embankment, watching the train go by. They do not move, and hence their world lines are simply vertical lines, each line at the particular distance between Cleveland and New York. On the other hand, there are people riding on that train. They move with the train, at a common (constant) speed. As seen from the embankment, their world lines are parallel slanted lines, the angle depending on the speed of the train. The persons standing on the embankment and those on the train have their *own* coordinate systems—in which they are not moving. In their own coordinate systems the world lines are vertical lines. But as seen from the others, they and their systems are moving; the world lines are slanted.

The world line of light will also be a straight line. Remember that nothing can move faster than light. Thus, it will give us the limit, the farthest edge of all world lines drawn from a point. At every world point of the Minkowski world, the totality of all directions in space and time forms a pencil of lines pointing away from the point. The lines form a cone, called a *light cone,* whose edges are formed by the world lines of light (fig. 10). There are two light cones, and, depending whether the lines point into the future or the past, they are referred to as the *future light cone* and the *past light cone,* respectively.

Consequences

Before the advent of relativity, the law of conservation of matter and the law of conservation of energy were ac-

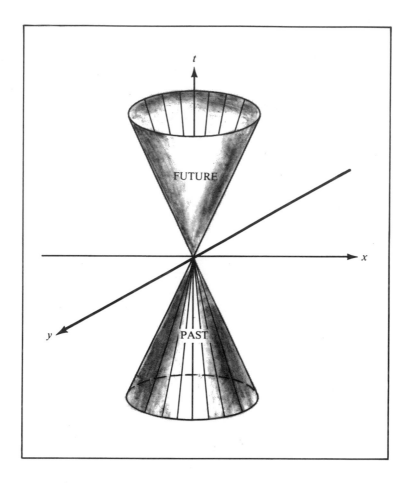

Figure 10.

cepted as two separate and independent laws. In other words, the total mass in the universe or in a closed system was to remain constant; similarly, the total energy was to remain unchanged. Einstein showed that mass and energy are inseparably linked together, that either could be converted into the other. The connection is provided by the famous *mass-energy relation*, $E = mc^2$. Here, E denotes the energy, m the mass, and c^2 the square of the speed of light.

It also shows that radiation, such as light, which has no mass, has an "effective mass" associated with it—its energy divided by the square of the speed of light. The stupendous result is that mass is energy and energy is mass. They are just two different forms of the same fundamental quantity, which is conserved. The equivalent energy of even a small amount of mass is tremendous. For example, the energy content of one gram of matter is equal to 2,860 kilowatt-years. Thus, at the cost of one gram of matter transformed into radiation, you could burn a 1,000-watt lamp for 2,860 years.

The truth of the above relation was demonstrated in the explanation of radioactivity, in which energy is produced constantly without any apparent source. It appears in nuclear reactions, in which the sum of the reacting masses, such as those of the target nucleus and the bombarding particle, is always greater than the sum of the resulting masses; the difference is released in the form of energy. It also plays a role in the explanation of the source of the immense amount of energy produced by the sun and stars—and in the frightful atomic explosions of Hiroshima and Nagasaki in Japan. Despite what you may have heard, Einstein never had anything to do with atomic energy or the production of atomic bombs. As a matter of fact, until the early thirties he never believed it could be done.

That time dilation was not just a wild dream was shown by the discovery of very fast, very small particles, called *mu mesons*. They are known to exist only for very short times, about 2 millionths of a second, after which they decay into electrons. Therefore, during their "lives" they travel at most 1,800 feet (600 m). Nevertheless, they have been found on Earth after traveling more than 4 miles (6,000 m) through the atmosphere. How is that possible? Their speed through the atmosphere is about 99.5 percent

the speed of light. At such great speeds our "clocks" and theirs differ very substantially, the relativistic time factor reaching the value 10. What is 2 millionths of a second to a mu meson appears to us to be 20 millionths of a second. If you were to ride on a mu meson, you would see things differently. The ride would indeed last only 2 millionths of a second and would cover 1,800 feet. However, as seen by us, the time elapsed is 20 millionths of a second and the distance covered, 180,000 feet (6,000 m). This makes it possible for us to find mu mesons way down at sea level, which could never occur without the large relativistic time dilation factor.

The most spectacular of the consequences of special relativity is the so-called twin paradox, which has caused a lot of unnecessary controversy. A paradox is a statement that may be true, but seems to say two opposite things. In fact, the twin paradox is no paradox at all but follows quite logically from what we said before. Only the conclusion is difficult to believe. Imagine identical twins, one remaining on Earth and the other traveling in a spacecraft at a speed nearly that of light. (Of course, no spacecraft can travel that fast—only mu mesons can.) Having reached his destination he turns around and, again at a speed nearly that of light, returns to Earth. If, according to his watch, the return trip has taken one year, his twin on Earth will say it took about seven years. In fact, the earthbound twin has aged seven years, but his brother is only one year older. How can this be? Did we not say that all observers

When an atomic bomb was dropped on Nagasaki, Japan, on August 9, 1945, the truth of Einstein's equation $E = mc^2$ was illustrated.

are equal, whether they are at rest or in motion? The twin who stayed on Earth could say: "My brother traveled to the right at nearly the speed of light and returned to me from the left." The space-traveling twin could say: "My brother was moving to the left at nearly the speed of light and then returned to me from the right." How can there be a discrepancy in the time they lived through? Except for the interchange of "left" and "right," the two statements are exactly the same.

This argument, in fact, is completely wrong. The situation is not symmetrical at all. If both brothers had traveled outward—in opposite directions—and then returned to Earth, it would be. But in our example, this was not the case. The twin who remained on Earth was constantly at rest in the same inertial frame of reference. Thus, his world line is a straight vertical one. On the other hand, we can find a reference system in which the space-traveling twin remained at rest, but it is not an inertial one. He was in one during his outward trip but then received a tremendous kickback that put him into another inertial frame. The alleged symmetry of his state with his brother's does not exist. His world line is a zigzag one, going first to one side, and then to the other, and finally meeting his brother's vertical one. From what we learned about world lines, it follows that the time that has elapsed for the twin who stayed at home is longer and that he has aged more than his brother.

Einstein's Recognition

It took some time before physicists—let alone the world at large—could get accustomed to these new ideas. The first scientist to see in Einstein's theory of relativity a more complete and truer picture of nature was Max Planck, the originator of *quantum theory*. He congratulated him on having given humanity a new understanding of nature's way, "which affected the very roots of our physical world." Slowly Einstein's fame spread, and he received a number of invitations to lecture. A special chair in theoretical physics was created at the University of Zurich, and Einstein was appointed to it after Friedrich Adler, a friend of his, withdrew because "Einstein's scientific powers were by far greater than mine." But he did not stay in Zurich long. In 1911 he was offered the position of "professor ordinarius" (full professor) at the German university in Prague, Czechoslovakia, then part of the Austro-Hungarian empire. He accepted, but his stay there was also to be short. In 1912 he returned to Switzerland, to the Federal Institute of Technology—to which he had come as a poor student sixteen years earlier and which had denied him an assistantship. Now he was a famous professor, and though students pushed, shoved, and jostled each other to get into his lectures, nothing had changed—he was still the easygoing and even untidy dreamer. However, Max Planck had been trying to get his friend one of the coveted positions at the Prussian Academy of Science in Berlin. In 1914 he succeeded, and Einstein could finally devote all his time to research, undisturbed by lectures, which he described as "performance on the trapeze." From the academy, while the world was embroiled in a war, came a message that will stand when World War I is long forgotten—the general theory of relativity.

5

GRAVITY
THE GENERAL
THEORY OF
RELATIVITY

The basic principle on which all our previous considerations were based is the principle of special relativity or, in other words, the equivalence of all inertial observers and inertial frames of reference. However, Einstein believed that there should be no distinction between *any* type of reference system—stationary, moving at constant speed, or even at varying speeds—and that it should be possible to formulate the laws of nature so as to preserve the equivalence of *all* frames of reference. We might call this the general principle of relativity.

We have seen that uniform—that is, unchanging—motion is relative. A person traveling by train at a constant speed could imagine that he is at rest and the embankment with the telephone poles and houses is moving in the opposite direction. Only the fact that he *knows* that the car is moving convinces him of his error. But if there were no windows in the car, he would not know whether he is moving or not. But acceleration, a change of speed, is a different matter—or so it seems. Suppose that the moving train stops (or at least slows down) when the engineer puts on the brakes. The occupants of the train will then experience a corresponding jerk forward. It would thus appear impossible to assume that the same physical laws apply to the nonuniform motion of both the train and the embankment. Yet, Einstein argued, if speed is relative, what is so unique about acceleration? Why should it be nonrelativistic, or absolute?

Einstein succeeded in showing that the equivalence of all frames of reference could be maintained in formulating the laws of nature, and in doing so "created" the general theory of relativity and, incidentally, a theory of gravitation. Just as his special theory of relativity is based on two postulates, so is the general theory of relativity, namely the principle of equivalence and the principle of covariance. However, before talking about them, we have to consider the nature of gravitation in more detail.

Gravitation and the Gravitational Field

If we drop a stone, it will fall to the ground. Why? The usual answer is, "Because it is attracted by the Earth." The force on the stone will produce an acceleration, which is the same for all objects falling freely, no matter what their shape or mass. There is a famous story, not necessarily true, of Galileo dropping objects from the Leaning Tower of Pisa to show that all objects, dropped or thrown, fall under gravity with the same acceleration (if we neglect air resistance). This acceleration turns out to be 32 feet (980 cm) per second per second.

Newton had shown that the same force that is responsible for attracting the stone to the Earth is also responsible for making the moon go around the Earth or all the planets revolve around the sun. It is a universal force that acts between any two bodies, attracting them to each other. (Not only does the Earth attract the stone, but also the stone attracts the Earth. However, because the mass of

Earth is so much greater than that of the stone, the effect on the Earth is quite negligible. This would not be so if the two objects attracting each other were of comparable mass.) This force of gravity, in Newton's theory, was an instantaneous action-at-a-distance force. But we know that, according to relativity, no signals can travel faster than light, nor could the gravitational effect be suddenly everywhere at a common, simultaneous instant. Newton himself was aware of this difficulty, and in a letter he wrote: "It is an absurdity to think that gravity should be innate, inherent and essential to matter, so that one body may act upon another at a distance through a vacuum without the mediation of anything else."

The idea of a *field* was already known from a study of electromagnetic phenomena. If, for example, a magnet attracts a piece of iron, we cannot accept the view that the magnet acts directly at a distance on the iron through the intervening empty space. Instead, we have to imagine that the magnet calls into being something physically real in the space around it, which we call the magnetic field. It is this field that, in turn, interacts with the iron, pulling it to the magnet. We can visualize this concept by placing iron filings on a piece of paper and a magnet under it. The iron filings will align themselves along the lines of force (fig. 11).They will be closer together at the poles, where the field is strong, and farther apart in the middle, where it is weak.

The same ideas can also be applied to, say, the attraction exerted by the Earth on a stone. Instead of talking about the force between the Earth and the stone, we introduce the notion of the *gravitational field*. This field is produced by the Earth and, in turn, interacts with the stone— or, more correctly, with the field produced by the stone. In practice, the latter is negligible. Thus, the stone will move in the Earth's gravitational field. Similarily, the at-

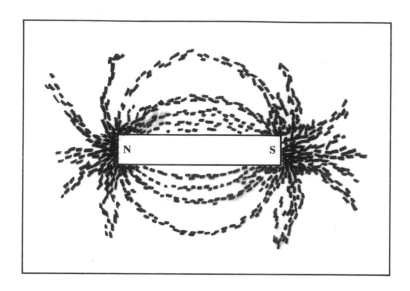

Figure 11.

traction between the sun and the planets, or the attraction between the Earth and the moon, can be expressed in terms of the actions of their respective gravitational fields. In general, any massive object produces a gravitational field, which in turn interacts with other masses and their gravitational fields. In contrast to electric and magnetic fields, however, gravitational fields exhibit another property not present in the others. Bodies moving under the sole influence of a gravitational field receive an acceleration that depends neither on the material nor the physical state of the body. For example, a piece of wood and a piece of lead will fall in exactly the same manner in a gravitational field (in empty space) when they start off from rest or with the same initial velocity (neglecting air resistance).

Acceleration is the change of speed with time. Therefore, if a body's speed is expressed as feet (or cm) per second, its acceleration, or change of speed per unit of time, will be expressed as feet (or cm) per second per second (sometimes as feet/sec [cm/sec] per sec).

Gravitation versus Acceleration

For a given constant mass, force is proportional to acceleration. If we double the force acting on a body, the acceleration will be twice as great. If we halve the force, the acceleration will be halved. However, the mass works in two different ways: We have already noted that objects dropped from a tower—or thrown into the air—will fall, owing to gravity, with the same acceleration. This is the *acceleration of gravity*, which determines the "weight" of a body. On the other hand, in the absence of gravity—in interstellar space—one can produce the same acceleration as that due to gravity by an equal force, such as that from a coiled spring. In that case the mass is called the *inertial mass*.

The equivalence of these two kinds of masses was known to Galileo and Newton. It was verified to an accuracy of one in one hundred million by the Hungarian physicist Count Roland von Eötvös and by R. Dicke and collaborators at Princeton in 1964 to a much higher degree of precision.* Mass was—and is—used both as a measure of the *inertia*, the tendency of a body to remain at rest or in uniform motion against forces, and to account for gravitational effects, namely weight (or heaviness). However, it was Einstein, with his infallible intuition, who realized that the equality of the two types of masses was no coincidence and that it provides the key to a deeper understanding of inertia and gravitation. The same quality of a

---

*Von Eötvös performed his experiments from 1889 to 1908, but they were only published posthumously in 1922.

body manifests itself, according to circumstances, as inertia or as weight. There is complete *equivalence* between gravitation and accelerated systems.

Imagine an elevator removed from gravity. Attached to its roof is a rope (fig. 12a). The elevator is now pulled upward with an acceleration of 32 feet (980 cm) per second per second, which is the acceleration of gravity—the same acceleration (but in the opposite direction) a body would have if it were dropped from a tower. An object,

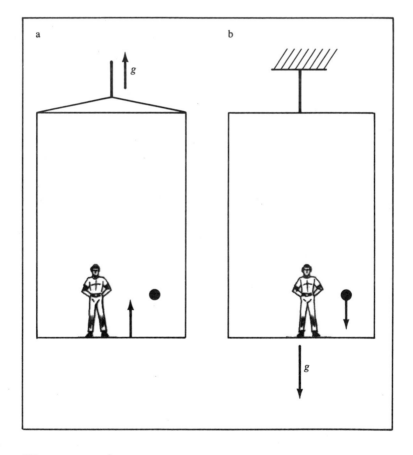

Figure 12a, b.

such as an apple, dropped in that elevator seems to reach the floor with the same acceleration of 32 feet per second per second. However, it is the floor that moves upward at the rate and meets the apple (which actually is at rest). You are in that elevator. Relying on your knowledge of gravity, you will come to the conclusion that you, the apple, and the elevator itself are being acted on by gravity and you are in a (constant) gravitational field (fig. 12). Looking up to the ceiling, you might see the hook to which the rope is attached, which keeps the elevator from falling. In the first instance we have an accelerated system of reference and an inertial mass; in the second there is a constant gravitational field and a gravitational mass. But since inertial mass equals gravitational mass, the two situations are equivalent. This, in essence, is what Einstein later called the *principle of equivalence*. It is an essential ingredient of the general theory of relativity. It permitted Einstein to find out what happened in the presence of a gravitational field. For this purpose he merely had to imagine what a uniformly accelerated observer would find in empty space. (Conversely, such an observer would be "replaced" by one in a constant gravitational field.)

Covariance

The equivalence principle was an important step forward, but Einstein was concerned about a more complex problem. Why should certain reference bodies (or their states of motion) be given priority over others (or their states of motion)? Nothing in classical mechanics justifies such a preference. Suppose an observer is in free fall toward the Earth. He will see a stone released suspended in the air instead of falling toward the ground—yet we know that the stone *is* falling toward the Earth with an acceleration of 32 feet per second per second. (The force of gravity still attracts the stone.) The observer's measurements, on the other hand, give an acceleration of *zero*—in contradiction to Newton's laws—since he himself is falling at that rate. Newton got around this difficulty by claiming that the laws of motion only hold if we are in the "right" frame of reference. If we move relative to that frame—except at constant speed—the validity of the law is destroyed. But what is so special about a particular frame of reference, or even a class of such frames (like the inertial frames)? After all, they are artificial devices, albeit convenient ones, in which measurements can be carried out. We should be free to choose any frame of reference we please and be assured that the laws of mechanics (in particular, the laws of motion) still hold. Such a situation can only be achieved in a physics that conforms to the general principle of relativity, since the equations of such a theory hold for every system of reference, whatever its state of motion.

The problem Einstein struggled with for some time was how to formulate the equations governing the laws of mechanics so that they would hold in an *arbitrary* reference system. They should have the same "form"—be invariant—in *any* system of coordinates. We say that equations written in this way are *generally covariant*.

In his search for a proper mathematical formulation, Einstein was aided by his old friend Marcel Grossmann, who pointed out that two Italian mathematicians, Ostillio Ricci and Tullio Levi-Civita, had developed a branch of mathematics, known as *tensor calculus,* which deals exactly with the problem of formulating equations in arbitrary coordinate systems. At this point the principle of equivalence enters the picture. The equivalence of gravitational field and accelerated systems of reference would guarantee that equations for the gravitational field in a covariant form would be valid in *any* system of reference. It had been known that Newton's universal law of gravitation could be expressed as one equation for the gravitational potential. To put them in a generally covariant form was another matter. But with the help of tensor calculus, Einstein succeeded. Instead of one equation for one gravitational potential in the Newtonian case, we now have equations for ten components of the gravitational potential. This is the price we had to pay to express the equations for the gravitational field in a generally convenient form. (Fortunately, of the ten quantities "only" six are independent, which can be further reduced by taking the symmetry of the problem into account.)

Gravitation and Geometry

The gravitational potentials were to play another important role. Let us recall that Minkowski interpreted Einstein's special theory of relativity as a new geometrical theory, in which space and time form a four-dimensional continuum. But the underlying geometry remains a Euclidean one, in which the coordinate axes are still straight lines at right angles to each other. The main difference lies in the fact that we now have four such axes, and that the invariant distance between two neighboring points involves the distance along the time axis as well as that of the space axes. However, even in nonrelativistic physics, Euclidean geometry is not the only possible one. For example, on a sphere (such as the Earth's surface), we use great circles *(meridians)* passing through the North and South poles and circles parallel to the equator as axes. The coordinate of a point is then given by its longitude (the meridian along which it lies, measured from a fixed one) and its latitude (its angular distance from the equator). The geometry is no longer that proposed by Euclid. For example, the sum of the angles in a triangle is no longer 180 degrees, as on a flat surface (fig. 13a), but larger than 180 degrees (fig. 13b). The "invariant" distance on that surface will also contain factors involving the angles.

The German mathematician Carl Friedrich Gauss considered the problem in general (while working on a government survey of Hanoverian lands). He found that it is possible to identify any point, *P,* on an arbitrarily curved surface uniquely by a pair of numbers, its *curvilinear coordinates.* This is possible even if the "coordinate axes" are arbitrarily bent lines, provided the lines of one system do not intersect each other and the lines of one system intersect all the lines of the other system. The distance between two neighboring points is given in terms of three functions that depend on the curvilinear coordinates, while the curvature is uniquely determined by these functions. Gauss had only considered surfaces, two-dimensional spaces. His ingenious student G.F.B. Riemann showed that these ideas could be generalized to spaces of any number of dimensions.

The geometry developed by Riemann, known as Riemannian geometry, suited Einstein's purposes perfectly. It was valid for all Gaussian-type coordinate systems, making it possible to formulate the laws of nature so as to preserve the equivalence of these general frames of reference. The invariant four-dimensional distance between two neighboring points, called the *line element,* involves ten quantities, which can vary from point to point and are known as the components of the *metric tensor.* The curvature is again uniquely determined by this tensor, except now—because of the larger number of dimensions—the curvature tensor has many more components. Only if all these components vanish will space be flat and can we retrieve the Minkowski world.

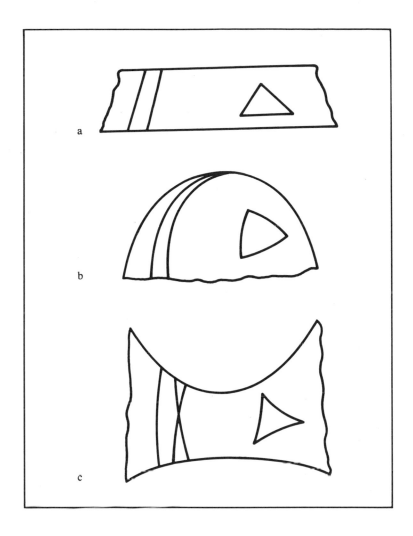

Figure 13. Plane surface (a): zero curvature, only one line can be drawn through a point, parallel to another straight line. Sum of angles in triangle equals 180°. Surface extends to infinity. Spherical surface (b): positive curvature, all great circles intersect. Sum of angles in triangle is larger than 180°. Surface is closed. Hyperbolic surface (c): negative curvature, many lines can be drawn through a point without intersecting others. Sum of angles in triangle is smaller than 180°. Surface is closed in the middle but open at ends.

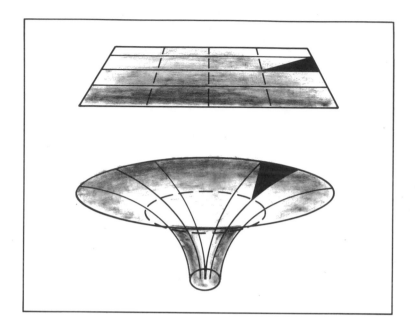

Figure 14. Top view: flat space. Bottom view: curved space in presence of matter (not shown). Similar to heavy object dropped on stretched rubber sheet.

It was at this point that Einstein's genius came to the fore. By identifying the metric tensor with the gravitational potential, he transformed gravitation into a geometrical theory. Gravitation now becomes a manifestation of the curvature of the underlying space. In the absence of a gravitational field, space is flat, or—in the language of reference systems—we have an inertial frame of reference. The presence of (large) masses produces a gravitational field—the connection being made via the field equations. The gravitational potential is then interpreted as the metric tensor, so that space-time will no longer be flat but "warped" or curved (fig. 14). The assumption of a special "gravitational force" now becomes superfluous. Objects move—such as the planets around the sun or a stone fall-ing—not because they are acted upon by the force of grav-ity but because they move along *geodesics,* the analogues of the shortest distance between points. It is as if they were "lazy" and followed the easiest possible path. It is the masses that determine the geometry of the world. In the absence of matter we have flat space; in the presence of matter space becomes curved, and particles as well as photons move along geodesics, which are those paths of "shortest distance" in the four-dimensional continuum.

change the shape of your ellipse by changing the length of the string or the distance between the pins.

Now, the ellipse described by Mercury—which is the planet closest to the sun—seems to shift. After a complete revolution the *perihelion*, the point closest to the sun, moves slightly forward. It only returns to its original position after 220,000 years. The result is a kind of rosette pattern (fig. 15). Part of the discrepancy was found to result from the closeness of other planets, such as Venus. But a small shift still remained unexplained. Not very much—it only amounts to forty-three seconds of arc every hundred years—

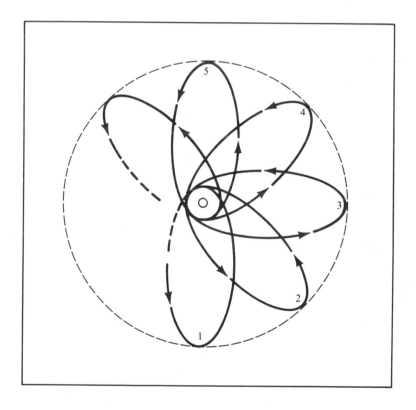

Figure 15. Planet motion indicated by unbroken lines, successive ellipses are numbered (highly exaggerated).

but scientists are very conscientious, especially when phenomena are not in agreement with theory. Several explanations were put forward. One was that the law governing the motion of planets should be changed slightly. Another was the presence of an unknown planet between the sun and Mercury. The "new" planet was even named—Vulcan. But nobody could show that it really existed. Now Einstein showed that, according to his theory, a small variation from Keplerian motion—which governs the motion of planets in their orbits—should take place. This variation would produce a shift of the perihelion of exactly the required amount—the missing forty-three seconds. "Imagine my joy," he wrote to a friend, when his equations yielded the correct perihelion motion of Mercury. "I was beside myself with ecstasy for days." (The other planets also have such perihelion shifts, but they are too small to be detected. The next planet, Venus, has an orbit that is nearly circular. Its perihelion, therefore, is difficult to locate exactly.)

Bending of Light

However, what made Einstein famous was his prediction of the bending of light by a gravitational field. Any theory can be tested experimentally by one of two methods. It has to explain known facts or predict new ones. Einstein did both. He explained the perihelion motion of Mercury. He predicted the bending of light by a gravitational field.

Though Einstein has realized much earlier that light would be bent by a gravitational field, to predict the exact amount of the deflection, he had to complete his calculations. Let us return for a moment to our elevator (fig. 12). Imagine a ray of light beamed across it. It travels in a straight line. But on account of the *upward* acceleration of the elevator it will seem to curve downward—as seen by

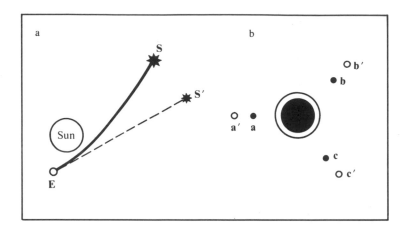

*Figure 16a. Star at S appears to be at S' as seen from Earth, E. Figure 16b. Actual position of stars: **a**, **b**, **c**, and as they appear when light is bent by the sun: **a'**, **b'**, **c'**. The sun (central black circle) is eclipsed by the moon; only a thin halo (white ring) remains.*

a person in the elevator. Now, the principle of equivalence tells us that the result must be the same if we replace the acceleration by a gravitational field. Therefore, light should be bent in a gravitational field.

To show this experimentally we need a large, heavy body—such as the sun—to produce a gravitational field. Light from a star close to the sun will then be bent "inward" as it passes the sun. But we—like a photographic camera—assume that light travels in straight lines. The star will therefore appear shifted "outward," away from the sun (fig. 16a). The shift is rather small, but it can be detected. The question is how. To find the *true* position of the star—when the sun is not there to deflect the light—is comparatively easy. The problem is to find the apparent—shifted—position, when the sun *is* there. The sun's light completely outshines that of any star in the vicinity. A way has to be found to block out the sun's light. This is possible only during a complete solar eclipse—when the moon comes between the sun and the Earth and its shadow touches the Earth—a rare event that can only be fully observed at a few places. On May 29, 1919, there was a solar eclipse—it would be total at Sobral in northeastern Brazil and at Principe Island, off the west coast of Africa. Expeditions were sent to these places.

For stars close to the edge of the sun (about one sun's radius away), the theory predicted a deflection of 1.73 seconds of arc, slightly larger if the star is closer to the sun and smaller if it is farther away (fig. 16b). It is interesting to note that Einstein's result is exactly twice the value predicted by Newtonian theory, the other factor resulting from the "curvature" of space produced by the sun. Comparison of the findings of the solar expeditions with those obtained six months earlier—when the sun was not there—confirmed Einstein's prediction exactly. On hearing the results Einstein wrote to his ailing mother—apparently to cheer her up—"Good news today . . . the British expeditions have actually proved the light deflection near the sun."*

World Fame

When the results of the solar eclipse observations became known to the general public, Einstein achieved fame. The story was front-page material for weeks, and Einstein's picture appeared all over the world. People who had never heard about gravity talked about Einstein's theory. Books and magazine and newspaper articles tried to make the

*Banesh Hoffmann and Helen Dukas. *Albert Einstein, Creator and Rebel.* New York: New American Library, 1973.

theory understandable to everyone. Einstein alone remained unperturbed by the general acclamation. He had only done his job as scientist—to search and to find—nothing more. Gigantic sums of money were offered to him for articles, pictures, and advertisements. He refused them all and continued to live the simple life he had led before. He was not a film star or prizefighter; publicity and money meant nothing to him. To friends who pointed out how much good he could do with the money, he replied:

> *I am absolutely convinced that no wealth in the world can help humanity forward. The example of great and fine personalities is the only thing that can lead us to fine ideas and noble deeds. Can anyone imagine Moses, Jesus or Gandhi with the money bags of Carnegie?*
>
> The World as I See It

He lived up to this belief. World War I had just ended, but the enmity among nations had not. Now Einstein appeared as the general messenger of peace and international understanding. Science is international; its language—mathematics—can be understood equally well by an Englishman, a Chinese, or an Italian. Nature's secrets are open to investigation by everyone, irrespective of race, sex, religion, or nationality. This was part of his message, and Einstein wrote, appeared on platforms, and addressed meeting after meeting. Although he was German by birth, his fame was universal. France and England rushed to honor him. He traveled to Japan, Palestine, and India—and was received with acclamation everywhere. In 1922, too, he received the Nobel Prize in physics. The Nobel Prize, the highest honor a scientist can receive, is given for outstanding work. Strangely enough, Einstein was awarded the prize not for his theory of relativity but for his early work on the photoelectric effect. Apparently, the prize committee wanted to avoid any complications. The subject of general relativity was still too controversial.

Reddening of Light

Not only will light be bent by a gravitational field, but its *frequency*—the number of oscillations per second—will also change. In order to understand this, let us return once more to our elevator (fig. 12.) Let us assume that there are two observers, one at the bottom (let us call him B) and one at the top (called T) of the elevator. Both are equipped with atomic clocks—that is, clocks whose "ticking" is produced by regularly emitted electromagnetic radiation. Because of the upward acceleration of the elevator, it will take longer for waves sent by B to reach T than it will for radiation emitted by T's clock to reach B. Thus, T will see B's clock going more slowly than his, while B will see T's clock going faster. By the principle of equivalence, this must also be true for an elevator in a gravitational field. Now, under certain conditions atoms emit radiation—energy in the form of light—at certain definite frequencies. (It is this fact that permits us to use atomic clocks.) Then, as Einstein had already pointed out in 1907, if we compare the frequencies of light reaching us from atoms, say, on the sun, with the frequencies of light from the same atoms situated on the earth, they will not be the same; those from atoms on the sun have a lower frequency. But lower frequency means "redder" light—the "spectrum" of the emitted radiation is shifted toward the red. For this reason the effect is called the *gravitational red shift*.

Except for very large or dense masses, the gravitational red shift is rather small and difficult to separate from a similar effect arising from the motion of the emitting object. In the case of the sun, for example, it is one part in half a million. However, it was definitely established by a beautiful experiment carried out at Harvard University in Cambridge, Massachusetts. The light emitted by an atom can be absorbed by another atom, if it is "tuned" to that frequency. The process is similar to the tuning of a radio or TV receiver to the exact frequency of the transmitter. When such light passes through a gravitational field—even one as weak as that of Earth—there is no absorption. The "receiver" has to be "retuned." It was found that light emitted from atoms situated at the top of a tower was received at a lower frequency than the one it had when emitted in accordance with Einstein's prediction.

More recently, an experiment was suggested that would make the curvature of space directly observable. A spinning gyroscope has the property that its axis always points in the same direction. It is this quality that makes it so useful for navigators. For some time now, it has been used instead of the magnetic compass on ships and airplanes. Suppose such a gyroscope is placed aboard a sattellite revolving around Earth. Its axis will point in the same direction with considerable steadiness. But on account of the assumed curvature of space resulting from Earth's gravitational field, the axis will move slightly—it will *precess,* that is, wobble or rotate—during each revolution of the satellite. The effect is rather small, only 7 seconds of arc per year. (If we recall that one degree has 60 minutes and one minute, 60 seconds, the axis will have turned two thousandths of one degree in one year.) For this reason the experiment is difficult to perform; moreover, there are other competing influences, such as the rotation of Earth, which have to be taken into account.

It should be mentioned that the experimental tests that have been described involve only comparatively small gravitational fields. Thus, the effects appear only as corrections to the classical, nonrelativistic results. It would be desirable to consider verifications involving large masses or strong gravitational fields (some of these "new developments" will be discussed in a later chapter); only then could one be absolutely sure that general relativity is the correct theory. As a matter of fact, modifications have been proposed, some of which also explain the above observations. However, none of them possesses the simplicity and beauty of Einstein's theory of general relativity—at least as far as the present author is concerned. But that does not mean that the general theory of relativity will not be superseded by an even more general theory. However, until such a theory is found (if at all), it is worth our while to consider applications and possible generalizations of general relativity.

THE 7
UNIVERSE

From the very start, as soon as he had obtained his gravitational equations, Einstein had intended general relativity to apply to the universe as a whole. But he had to test the theory first on a local scale. The deflection of light by the gravitational field of the sun and the perihelion motion of Mercury had shown that the theory of general relativity predicted the correct results.

Classical celestial mechanics, as derived from Newton's theory of gravitation, was not consistent with observation. The *universe*, the cosmos, consists of clusters of galaxies; galaxies consists of clusters of stars, dust, and radiation. *Galaxies* are huge collections of billions of stars; more than a thousand trillion galaxies can be seen in the largest telescopes. Our sun is part of such a galaxy, usually referred to as the *Milky Way*, because of the way it appears in a clear night sky. On a large scale the matter in the universe may be considered to be distributed uniformly. Since it had been assumed that the universe is infinite, both in respect to space and time, you would find the same distribution of stars everywhere, no matter how far you might travel through space.

However, if the density (that is, the number of stars per unit of volume) is the same throughout, then according to Newton's theory the force of gravitation acting on a star at the surface of a sphere containing the matter would become infinitely large as the radius of that sphere keeps increasing. But this is impossible; hence the density must decrease as the distance (radius) increases, with fewer and fewer stars until finally there would only be empty space—but this is contrary to observation.

Einstein, also, was not successful at first in solving this riddle. When he applied his equations for the gravitational field to infinite space filled with a uniformly distributed matter, he could not make it fit at infinite distances, no matter how hard he tried. Now, in his usual daring manner, he took a bold step. If the theory was not consistent with infinite space, then space could not be infinite in extent. After ''rather a rough and winding road,'' he arrived at a remarkable conclusion: The universe is finite (closed) in its spatial dimensions (length, width, and breadth) —finite but without boundaries. If you traveled far enough in any direction, you would return to the original point of departure. Such a universe can be likened to the surface of a sphere, which is closed but without boundaries. Traveling, for example, along a meridian on the surface of the Earth—a circle passing through the North and South poles—one would, after a complete circumnavigation, arrive again at the point of departure, but one could go on forever without reaching any boundaries.

Closed but Unbounded

Einstein's idea can best be illustrated by considering a two-dimensional world—that is, one having only length and width but not thickness—such as a plane. The inhabitants of that world also have only length and width, as do their

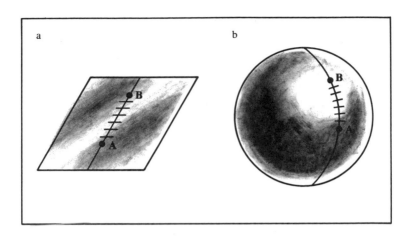

Figure 17a. Two-dimensional beings measure distance between points A and B along their "straight line."
Figure 17b. On the surface of a sphere, a "straight line" is an arc of a great circle.

measuring rods. For them nothing exists outside "their" plane. They can measure distances in the usual fashion by laying their measuring rods end to end in a straight line (fig. 17a). They can travel on the plane indefinitely—until they fall off, unless the plane is infinite in extent.

Now, take a different type of world, still a two-dimensional one, but one no longer flat such as the surface of a sphere. The whole universe for the inhabitants of this world extends exclusively over this surface. They will measure distances along lines that are no longer straight but curved and that we "three-dimensional beings" call part of a great circle (fig. 17b). The charm of this world is that the universe of these beings is finite and yet has no limits. If they want to go on a "world tour" of their universe, they can just go on and on in what they would call a straight line but really is the arc of a great circle, returning to their starting point at the end of the tour. Yet they do not have to go on such a world tour to find out that their world is not flat. If they draw three "straight" lines intersecting each other, they will get a "triangle." The sum of the three angles of a triangle in plane geometry is 180 degrees. For a spherical surface, they will find the sum to be *greater* than 180 degrees, while for a hyperbolic (saddle-shaped) surface the sum will be *smaller* than 180 degrees (see figure 13). They are thus able to determine the kind of surface they live on, even if only a small part of their universe is available for their measurements. However, if this part is very small, they will not be able to distinguish between a flat and curved universe because a small part of a spherical universe differs only slightly from a piece of a plane of the same size. Thus, if those beings live on a small part of a spherical universe, they have no way of determining whether they are living in a finite or infinite universe, because that part of the universe which is available for their measurements is in both cases practically flat.

There exists a three-dimensional analogy to this two-dimensional spherical universe. Just as on a sphere all points are equivalent (that is, the same distance from the center), so all points in the three-dimensional spherical universe are equivalent. Just as the two-dimensional spherical universe is finite and has a finite "area" depending on the radius, so a three-dimensional spherical universe is finite and has a finite "volume" depending on the radius. Just as two-dimensional beings traveling on a spherical surface will reach their starting point after a complete circumnavigation, so we three-dimensional beings traveling on a *hypersphere,* as this three-dimensional surface is called, will reach our original position after a complete circuit.

We don't know whether we live in an infinite (flat or open) universe or in a finite (closed) one. The part of the universe that we can see is just too small to make such a determination. However, closed spaces without limits are conceivable, and the difficulties in connection with the Newtonian universe—density decreasing or gravitational forces increasing toward the boundary—disappear. To this three-dimensional space Einstein now added a fourth dimension—time. It is uncurved and infinite, from the distant past to the distant future. This, then, is the world we live in: finite in its space dimensions, but infinite in time.

The Expanding Universe

Einstein's universe was a static one. Matter was believed to be distributed uniformly and the same for all time. This also corresponded to the observations made then. The stars indeed appeared to be fixed and nonmoving in space. Not only was Einstein's universe uniformly populated by stationary matter, its size—and radius—remained the same for all time. It may be likened to a giant raisin cake of fixed size, whose many raisins, like the stars, remain fixed in space.

Only a few years later, the Russian mathematician Alexander Friedmann noted that Einstein's equations admitted time-dependent solutions, even under the strict conditions of homogeneous matter distributed uniformly. Friedmann's universe still was uniformly populated, but it could expand (or contract) like a balloon that is being blown up (or deflated). As a matter of fact, there are three types of Friedmann universe, depending on whether the gravitational attraction of the matter can or cannot overcome the initial expansion, which is believed to be due to an explosion. If the gravitational attraction is strong enough— that is, if there is enough matter in the universe—the universe will continue to expand until it reaches a certain maximum size at which the two opposing interactions— gravitation and expansion—balance, after which gravitation takes over and it will contract. According to a strict mathematical interpretation of Friedmann's solution, it will contract to the original zero radius and then start to expand again, producing a kind of oscillation. This is physically not realistic, and one would expect other processes to occur before the original state is reached, starting another cycle of expansion and contraction. On the other hand, if the gravitational attraction is not strong enough to overcome the expansion—that is, if there is not enough matter in the universe—the universe will expand and continue to expand forever. In the first case this will result in a closed universe and in the second, in an open universe. There is also a flat universe, which will also continue to expand, but at a slower rate. This is similar to a rocket fired from Earth. If its initial speed is smaller than a certain "critical" speed, the *escape velocity,* it will remain a captive of Earth's gravitational attraction and will eventually fall back to Earth. On the other hand, if its speed is equal to or greater than the escape velocity, it will escape. If, instead of Earth, we consider a larger and heavier body, such as the planet Jupiter, the escape velocity will also be larger, so that a rocket that can get away from Earth might not be able to escape from Jupiter. At present we do not know exactly how much matter there is in the universe or whether it is large enough to overcome the expansion. All we know is that now and for millions of years to come, the universe is expanding.

At first Friedmann's new solution was considered to be a mathematical oddity, without any observational corroboration. The stars appeared to be fixed in space and nonmoving. Only much later was it shown that this is not so.

You may have noticed that the whistle of a train approaching a station seems to be shriller, to have a higher pitch, than that of one leaving it. This is due not to increasing loudness but to an apparent change in *frequency,* the number of waves emitted per second. When the train is approaching, more of the sound waves are crowded into a shorter distance. Hence the frequency, the number of waves reaching you per second, is higher and the tone shriller. Similarly, when the train is moving away, the distance is growing. The frequency is lower and the pitch, the shrillness, is lower (fig. 18). It is the same with light waves. If a star is moving away from us, the frequency of the light waves we receive is decreased. But the frequency determines the color of the light we see; lower frequency means redder light and higher frequency more bluish light.

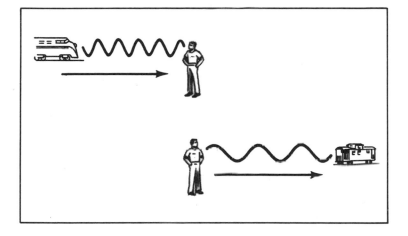

Figure 18. Doppler Effect: the observed pitch or frequency increases as a train approaches (above), since more waves are crowded into a shorter distance. It will decrease when the train is moving away (below), since the available length is longer (although the number of waves emitted remains unchanged).

We also know that atoms emit light of characteristic frequencies. If the star containing these atoms is receding, moving away, the light will seem to be "redder" than the light we would receive if it were standing still. Earlier we talked about another red shift, the gravitational red shift, which is due to atoms being in a stronger gravitational field than that of the observer. Now we are talking about another kind of red shift, due to the recession, or moving away, of stars. This red shift is called the *Doppler red shift* and is usually much larger than the gravitational red shift.

The American astronomer Edwin Hubble compared the red shifts of different galaxies with their distances from us and thus demonstrated that the galaxies are receding. He found that the red shifts were proportional to the distances. Galaxies that are farther away have larger red shifts than those close by. Those twice the distance have double the red shift, those three times the distance triple the red shift, and so on. Now, the red shifts themselves are related to the speed of recession. Larger red shifts mean larger speeds, with the same simple relation as for distances. Hubble concluded that the speed of recession is itself related to the distance in a simple manner. Stars (or galaxies) at twice the distance will have twice the speed and stars at three times the distance, three times the speed of those at a given distance, and so on. This relation is called *Hubble's law,* and the quantity relating distance and speed of recession is called *Hubble's constant.** Not only does it prove that the universe is expanding but also that the expansion is uniform. Only the distances between galaxies change, not their relative positions to each other—that is, the angles they make with each other (fig. 19).

*The term *constant* is somewhat misleading, since Hubble's constant can depend on time.

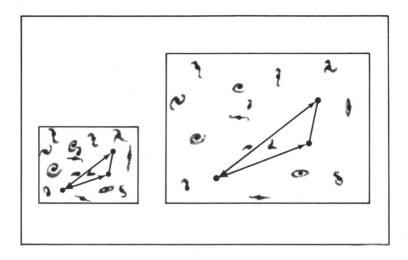

Figure 19. The universe at two stages of expansion. According to Hubble's law, the positions of galaxies relative to each other remain unchanged.

The fact that every galaxy is receding from us seems to say that we—our galaxy, the Milky Way—are at the center of the universe. But the opposite is the case. Every galaxy, including our own, is "running away" from every other galaxy. No single galaxy can be said to be the center of the universe. Consider a rubber balloon with buttons fixed to its surface. As the balloon is inflated, the distances between the buttons increase and the buttons seem to move away from each other (fig. 20). In the same way, as our universe expands, the galaxies move away from each other. An observer on any galaxy will see *all* other galaxies moving away. The universe has no center, only a (uniform) distribution of galaxies receding from each other at speeds proportional to their distances from each other. As a result of Friedmann's and Hubble's work, these models are now accepted as representative of the behavior of the universe—at least, as good approximations.

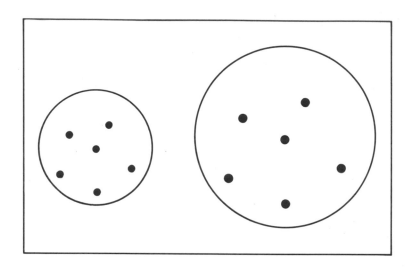

Figure 20.

In the Beginning

If the universe is continuously expanding—and its matter-energy content remains the same—then at some time in the distant past it must have been extremely small and dense. Extrapolating farther back, we arrive at a "singular state" of infinite density and zero volume. Such a situation can be envisaged mathematically but physically it is intolerable. Clearly, something quite unusual must have happened.

In 1965 two radio astronomers, Arno Penzias and Robert W. Wilson, at the Bell Laboratory in Murray Hill, New Jersey, set out to measure the radio waves emitted by our galaxy with their very sensitive "horn antenna" (plate 3). To their surprise, they found it to be considerably "hotter" (that is, absorbing more radiation) than expected. No matter how hard they tried to eliminate any extraneous effects, they found a persistent and uniform *background* *radiation* of about 3° Kelvin (about −270° C).* Moreover, when they plotted the intensity of that radiation against frequency, they found that the data fit the curve that could be expected from *black-body radiation* at that temperature. (A *black body* is an idealized substance that completely absorbs all radiation falling on it—without reflecting any—until it reaches a temperature at which it emits radiation at the same rate at which it receives it and continues to do so.) It should be noted that a black body is "black" in the sense that it is opaque, or nontransparent, and nonreflecting for radiation of all frequencies. For all practical purposes, stars can be considered to radiate energy as black bodies do, since they consist of very hot opaque gases that absorb radiation very effectively.

A reasonable explanation, then, is that this radiation is the residue of the original radiation emanating from the "fireball" of the initial explosion, commonly referred to as the *big bang*. Such a process, indeed, already had been suggested much earlier by George Gamow and his coworkers. In a paper humorously known as the alpha-beta-gamma paper (after the names of the authors: R. Alpher, Hans Bethe, and George Gamow), it was suggested that the universe started from a hot and very dense mass of *neutrons*, uncharged particles as heavy as protons (into which they decayed with the emission of electrons), submerged in a "sea" of high-energy radiation. (Gamow called this mixture *ylem*—defined as the "first substance from which the elements were supposed to be formed.") The original high-energy and high-temperature radiation would still be present, although, of course, at a much lower tem-

---

*The Kelvin scale is similar to the Centigrade one, except that its zero, where all thermal motion is supposed to cease, corresponds to −273.2° C. Thus, 0° C = −273.2° K.

perature, which Gamow estimated to be 5°. The theory was not quite correct, since the elements could not have been formed as predicted. However, the most remarkable thing is that the theory *did* predict the presence of a background radiation—and nobody bothered to look for it until it was discovered more or less by accident.

"In the Beginning There Was an Explosion."

It was an explosion, not like one familiar to us—which starts from a center and spreads out, engulfing more and more of the surroundings—but one that started everywhere, filling all of "space"—which, we recall, was extremely small—with matter and radiation. We can only speculate about what occurred when the density was nearly infinite and the gravitational forces were strong—even stronger than the "strong forces" that hold the nucleus together. A fraction of a second later the universe expanded and "cooled" down to a temperature of 100,000,000,000° C. This is so hot that no matter—molecules, atoms, or even the nuclei of atoms—could have held together. Instead, the universe was filled with a mixture of radiation and *elementary particles* colliding with each other. Such particles are *electrons,* negatively charged particles of small mass, and their counterparts, *positrons,* positively charged particles of the same mass. (If those two collide, they "annihilate," that is, destroy, each other and produce *photons,* the neutral carriers of electromagnetic radiation. Conversely, a positron-electron pair can be "created" by the collision of two photons.) In addition, there were neutrinos, particles with no mass or electric charge whatsoever. Also present were a smaller number of protons, positively charged particles about 1,800 times as heavy as electrons (or positrons), and neutrons, neutral particles about as heavy as protons. (Protons and neutrons are the building blocks of atomic nuclei, the lightest one being the nucleus of the hydrogen atom, which consists of just one proton.) As the expansion continued, the temperature dropped, reaching 10,000,000,000° C after one second. This was cool enough for electrons and positrons to annihilate faster than they could be formed, the energy released slowing down the rate of cooling temporarily. It was still too hot for neutrons and protons to combine into atomic nuclei, however, their ratio then being 24 percent neutrons and 76 percent protons. After about three minutes the temperature dropped to 1,000,000,000° C, cool enough for atomic nuclei to form, starting with deuterium (or heavy hydrogen), consisting of one proton and one neutron. Further collisions with neutrons and protons finally resulted in nuclei of *helium,* the most stable light nucleus, consisting of two protons and two neutrons. Not much of interest happened during the next few hundred thousand years, except that more matter was formed from radiation and the universe continued to expand and to cool. It then reached a temperature low enough for electrons and nuclei to combine to form atoms of hydrogen and helium. (The hydrogen atom has one electron and one proton, while the helium atom has two electrons outside its nucleus.) Under the influence of gravity the resulting gas would form into lumps, which would ultimately condense into stars and galaxies. Today, about twenty billion years later, we see the result. One hundred billion galaxies, each containing about one hundred billion stars, blanket the night sky and are still rushing away from each other as the universe continues to expand.

It is a plausible story, supported not only by the three-degree background radiation but also by measurements of the abundance of helium in the universe. But the fundamental question of where it all came from still has to be answered. How it will end, whether the universe will continue to expand forever or start to contract again, is yet another question. The answer must await telescopes that can probe farther into space and, because the light has taken a long time to travel these immense distances, also farther into the past.

When Adolf Hitler came to power in Germany, Einstein was visiting the California Institute of Technology in Pasadena, California. He refused to return to Germany but instead went to Le Coq-sur-Mer in Belgium. There he was guarded day and night because of threats on his life. When German emissaries urged him to return, he issued the following manifesto:

> *As long as I have any choice, I will only stay in a country where political liberty, tolerance, and equality of all citizens before the law prevail. Political liberty implies the freedom to express one's political opinions orally and in writing; tolerance implies respect for any and every individual opinion.*
>
> *These conditions do not obtain in Germany at the present time. . . .*
>
> Ideas and Opinions

In turn, the German press accused him of spreading atrocity stories and of warmongering. The Prussian Academy of Science, which had been so glad to receive Einstein in

1914, planned to expel him—on April 1, 1933, the day of a boycott against Jews—an action that he forestalled by resigning his membership, "being unable to serve the Prussian State under the present government."

Einstein received offers from universities in other countries to join their faculties. He finally accepted a position at the Institute for Advanced Study in Princeton, New Jersey, where he remained the rest of his life. He soon came to like the United States, which made him forget some of the troubles of being a refugee in a foreign country; and the United States liked the scientist, who was so amiable and so unconventional. Passersby in Princeton could often see strolling through the streets an elderly gentleman with long white hair, engrossed in his thoughts and completely oblivious to his surroundings. It was Einstein, of course.

An Unfulfilled Dream

In his special theory of relativity, Einstein gave new meaning to electrodynamics. He showed that there was no need for the ether: The electromagnetic field alone was the carrier of light and electromagnetic waves. In the general theory of relativity he showed that gravitation was "just geometry," with the masses determining the geometry of the world—flat space in the absence of matter and curved space where there was matter.

In Princeton, Einstein continued his work, devoted almost exclusively to an extension of his theory. He wanted to arrive at a unifying principle that would govern the na-

Einstein in his later years at Princeton

ture of the universe. It was an ambitious project. He spent the rest of his life, alone or with assistants, working on a *unified field theory,* which would bring together the concepts of gravitation, electromagnetism, and the more recent quantum phenomena as consequences of *one* system of equations. Others gave up, but not Einstein. "I need more mathematics," he said and continued. He was ridiculed by his colleagues, but he persisted. It was an obsession, a magnificent obsession, and only his death in 1955 stopped him from continuing his work. Einstein and others have made important contributions, but the ultimate solution—and many believe that there is one—still eludes us. The unified field theory is still an unfulfilled dream.

Einstein's basic idea is really simple. There is the electromagnetic field and there is the gravitational field. Each is governed by a set of equations. Each behaves in a similar way, decreasing in strength as the square of the distance. Why should there not be *one* set of equations governing *both* fields? Indeed, why not? Most physicists would agree with that, but Einstein demanded that we start from the relativistic theory of gravitation. That theory has demonstrated conclusively that the laws of nature are covariant under arbitrary transformations of coordinates. Therefore, from the beginning, the laws will have to possess covariance, which is only guaranteed by general relativity or its generalization.

Einstein and others proposed theories that satisfied this requirement and did unite gravitation and electromagnetism in one system of equations. One of his more promising theories is based on the simple fact that by giving up the symmetry of the metric tensor it could describe not only gravitation but also electromagnetism. As we saw earlier, the symmetric metric tensor has ten components that Einstein had identified as the ten gravitational potentials. On the other hand, electromagnetism can be described by six (antisymmetric) field quantities, three for the electric field and three for the magnetic field. Upon removing the symmetry of the metric tensor, it then contains sixteen components, or field quantities. If ten combinations of these are used for gravitation, the remaining six are just sufficient for describing electromagnetism.

You may wonder why, if any of those theories did unify gravitation and electromagnetism into one system of equations, they were not satisfactory. Let Einstein answer this himself: "It may well be true that this system of equations is reasonable from a logical standpoint, but this does not prove that it corresponds to nature. Experience alone can decide on truth." But Einstein always found some flaw in his equations—or in those of others. Solutions were found that showed that the theory could have no physical significance or they led to incorrect motions; charged particles would move as if they had no charge, and so on. In addition, Einstein's plan was even more ambitious. He wanted both matter *and* electric charges to be described by the geometry. To put it one way: The "left-hand side" of the field equations of general relativity describes the gravitational field, while the "right-hand side" contains the sources responsible for that field, matter, and other fields. Now, Einstein argued that for a pure unified field theory there should be no "right-hand side" of the equations; matter should enter as a part of the field itself. And that he was unable to do. He did show that the equations governing the motions of particles followed from his equations and did not have to be added as in Newton's theory of gravitation. But that, too, was not enough. He also hoped to obtain restrictions on the solutions that would correspond to the existence of atoms and quanta. It was a formidable task, even for Einstein. In formulating his general theory of relativity he had been guided by the principle of equivalence and the requirement of covariance, but here there was nothing except the strong conviction that such a unification should be possible to achieve. Against those odds even Einstein's remarkable intuition proved inadequate, and he was unable to fulfill his life's dream—a unified field theory.

Quantum Mechanics and Reality

Although Einstein's principal concern was general relativity and later the unified field theory, he did not abandon an active interest in the other great development of physics in this century, quantum theory and its offshoot, *quantum mechanics* (or wave mechanics). He criticized the latter for not giving a complete description of nature, and his hope was that the unified field theory would also explain quantum phenomena.

"God does not play dice with the world," which sums up Einstein's view of quantum mechanics, has become a famous line. Einstein felt that only our ignorance and, in particular, our interaction with the measuring apparatus prevent us from giving a complete description of the phenomenon. "Quantum mechanics is certainly imposing," he wrote, "but an inner voice tells me that it is not yet the real thing. The theory says a lot, but does not really bring us any closer to the secret of the Old One."

Most physicists—except Einstein, Erwin Schrödinger, and Planck, the originator of quantum theory—accepted the *Copenhagen doctrine,* as Niels Bohr's statistical interpretation of quantum mechanics became known. But it was only Einstein who, "along a lonely road," kept searching for a way to arrive at a model of reality that represents events themselves and not merely the probability of their occurrence. At no point did he deny or disparage the important successes of quantum theory or its logical consistency. "Quantum mechanics undoubtedly represents a major advance, but it is a restricted case of a future theory"—in the same way Newtonian mechanics is related to general relativity. "In order to arrive at such a theory one should not start with . . . quantum theory and try to fit it to general relativity" (that is, make it covariant). "Instead one should start with a unified field theory, and demand that the quantum rules should start with a unified field theory, and demand that the quantum rules should emerge as 'constraints.' " These constraints would result from overdetermining the fields. In the usual situation the number of unknown fields is equal to the number of equations necessary to determine them. If the number of unknowns is greater than the number of equations, then the fields are *underdetermined,* and we can choose some at will. However, if the number of unknowns is *smaller* than the number of equations, then the fields are *overdetermined,* and the extra equations will act as restrictions or constraints on the fields. It was Einstein's hope that those extra conditions should then emerge as the required quantum rules, but he failed to realize it. In his later years he even began to doubt whether it could be done. "It appears dubious whether a field theory can account for the atomistic structure of matter and radiation as well as of quantum phenomena," he wrote only a month before his death. However, "the aspiration to truth is more precious than its assured possession."

The Last Years

When it appeared that the Germans might be able to produce an atomic bomb, Einstein wrote—on the suggestion of his friends—to President Franklin D. Roosevelt, pointing out the feasibility of using nuclear energy. This was the total extent of Einstein's involvement in the Manhattan Project, the code name for the subsequent American effort to develop nuclear weapons during World War II. Later, Einstein wrote again urging that the bomb not be used. The letter arrived too late, however, and on August 6 and 9, 1945, the United States exploded atomic bombs over Hiroshima and Nagasaki, Japan. From that time on, Einstein and other leading scientists spearheaded a drive to inform the public as well as the politicians of the full impact of nuclear energy. This was not the total extent of his involvement in public affairs. Whenever he saw a worthwhile cause—for civil liberties or aid to refugees or to help his people—Einstein spoke out. Like a prophet of old, he condemned injustice whenever and wherever he saw it.

After the death in 1952 of Dr. Chaim Weizmann, the first president of Israel, Einstein was offered the presidency. Although deeply moved by the offer, he declined, pointing out that he lacked "both the natural aptitude and experience to deal properly with people and to exercise official functions." He believed that these reasons alone, not even mentioning his preoccupation with his work, would make him unsuited for that high office.

> *I am the more distressed over these circumstances because my relationship with the Jewish people has become my strongest human bond, ever since I became fully aware of our precarious situation among the nations of the world.*
> (from a letter to Abba Eban)

For years Einstein had been suffering from a dilation in the abdominal aorta. Only Einstein and his close friends knew how seriously ill he was. To everyone else he was his usual charming self, continuing to work—naturally—on the unified field theory. On April 18, 1955, Einstein died, his uncompleted calculations next to his bed, only a few months before the first of a series of international conferences on general relativity, which—instead of honoring the living man—became a memorial to his greatness.

AFTER 9
EINSTEIN

More than fifty years have passed since Einstein formulated the general theory of relativity. Many have trod the path he blazed. During the last twenty years there have been important advances in understanding the nature of our universe—partly due to improved technology.

Radioastronomy has provided us with a new and better "window" on the sky, making it possible to detect quasars, quasi-stellar radio sources that emit energy at a tremendous rate, and *pulsars,* rapidly pulsating radio sources. A theoretical study of gravitational collapse has given us insight into the end products of stellar evolution, leading to *neutron stars,* stars made up of highly compressed neutrons, *white dwarfs,* small "white" stars of high density, and even *black holes,* gravitationally collapsed stars. Progress has been made in the detection of gravitational waves emitted by massive bodies undergoing acceleration.

Einstein's unfulfilled dream of a unified field theory has been revived, together with work on a quantum theory of gravitation. From a mainly theoretical—and sometimes overlooked—field of study, relativity and its ramifications have advanced to the frontiers of physics and astronomy.

Unfortunately, limitations of "space-time" do not permit us to discuss here little more than one of the more spectacular consequences of the general theory of relativity—black holes.

The Schwarzschild Radius

Shortly after Einstein published his famous paper on general relativity in 1916, the first exact solution of his equations was given by Karl Schwarzschild, a German astronomer. It corresponds to the gravitational field outside a spherical mass, at large distances from it, exhibiting the correct inverse-square behavior of Newtonian gravitation. It remains *the* "classical" solution of Einstein's field equations. Associated with that solution is a certain distance, the *Schwarzschild radius,* which is, in fact, a measure of the object's gravitational mass and determines the curvature of the space. The larger the mass, the larger the radius and the more curved the underlying space.

We can visualize the Schwarzschild radius in a somewhat different manner. We have already seen that in order to enable a rocket to get away from the Earth or any other massive stellar object, it must have an initial speed larger than a critical speed, the escape velocity. In the case of Earth, the escape velocity is 6.8 miles (11 km) per second; that is, only if the rocket has a speed exceeding 6.8 miles per second will it be able to leave Earth forever. Suppose now that we could somehow compress Earth (but, of course, not changing its mass) to a fourth of its size; the escape velocity would then be 13.6 miles (22 km) per second, twice its previous value, and a rocket would now need that speed to coast away from Earth.

Further compressions will result in corresponding increases in the escape velocity. If we succeed in reducing

Earth's circumference to 2.176 inches (5.58 cm), the escape velocity will be 186,000 miles (300,000 km) per second—the speed of light. Now only light can escape from Earth. One last little squeeze, and the escape velocity *exceeds* the speed of light. Now nothing—not even light—can escape from Earth's surface. Contact between Earth and the rest of the universe has been permanently broken. Earth has become a black hole in space, with a circumference of 2.176 inches.

The word *black* in this context is used as in "black body," an object that absorbs all radiation including light. We see an object by the light it emits or reflects. A body will appear red when it absorbs all light except red light, which it reflects; it will look blue when only blue light is reflected. It will be white when it reflects all colors and black when it absorbs all colors. In practice only a black body (or a black hole) is "perfectly black" and is invisible. Outside the horizon, the edge of the "hole," the escape velocity is less than the speed of light, and very powerful rockets can still get away. Inside the horizon the escape velocity is greater than the speed of light and nothing can escape. The interior of the hole is completely cut off from the rest of the universe.

We thus see that the Schwarzschild radius is that region for which the escape velocity is equal to the speed of light. As long as the dimensions of actual stars are larger than their Schwarzschild radius—the usual situation—there is no problem; the Schwarzschild radius remains well within the body of the star. (For example, the sun's Schwarzschild radius is only about a mile.) However, if the star collapses, the "radius" of the contracting object will eventually become equal to—or smaller than—its own Schwarzschild radius (fig. 23). The main difference between the above hypothetical example and the actual situation in contracting stars is that for the Earth to become a black hole, external forces have to be applied; for a star to become a black hole, the necessary forces are supplied by its own internal gravity.

Gravitational Collapse

Of the forces of nature that hold atoms and nuclei together, gravitation is the weakest. But on the astronomical scale, where immense numbers of atoms and very large distances are involved,* the gravitational attractions of these atoms combine into one gigantic pull overwhelming all other forces. These either act only between charged particles, as do electromagnetic forces, or have a short range, as do the forces that keep nuclei together. In the universe, gravity is the dominant force, and gravitational collapse, the tendency of material bodies to gravitate toward a common center, is the main process.

Stars radiate heat and light and thus lose energy. As energy is released the star contracts, the temperature increases, and nuclear fuel is burned. That nuclear fuel results from nuclear reactions, whereby protons are "fused" together to form helium nuclei, with release of energy. As a result the star releases more energy and continues to shine for millions and billions of years, until its nuclear fuel runs out. With its fires quenched it can no longer stand up against the inward pull of its own gravity. Gravity wins the tug-of-war, and the star collapses.

White Dwarfs

What happens now depends on the mass of the star. If its mass is smaller than or equal to about 1.5 solar masses, it

---

*For example, our sun contains 10^{57} atoms (a one followed by fifty-seven zeros), a quantity so immense that it is unimaginable.

is "saved" from total collapse. Pressures, such as those that make it difficult to compress rocks, build up and balance the gravitational inward pull, thus halting the collapse. The star becomes a white dwarf. Gravitational forces compress its mass to a size even smaller than that of the Earth—hence the name *dwarf*—resulting in densities exceeding many tons per cubic centimeter. In the process, electrons are stripped from the atomic nuclei, forming a "degenerate gas" (the electrons in this "gas" behave more like a solid, being able to withstand large gravitational forces better than ordinary matter). Yet these stars have a very high surface temperature of about 24,000° K, emitting white light—hence the name *white dwarf*. White dwarfs are quite common in our galaxy, the average distance between them being about ten light-years. (A light-year is the distance light travels in one year, that is, about 60,000 times the distance of the Earth from the sun—or 6 trillion miles.) Our sun will eventually end up as a white dwarf, but this will take a few billion years, so we do not have to worry about it.

Neutron Stars

If the mass of the collapsing star is larger than 1.5 solar masses, the degenerate electron gas cannot withstand the huge gravitational forces, and the star continues to collapse rapidly. However, if the exploding star has a mass smaller than or equal to about 3 to 5 solar masses (the exact figure is still in doubt) or manages to get rid of its excess above that amount, it may still escape final collapse. When the density is a million times larger than that of a white dwarf, the nuclei themselves are affected as well as the electrons. The positively charged protons absorb the electrons, forming a "degenerate gas" of neutrons. It is this degenerate neutron gas that is able to withstand the much larger gravitational attraction due to the additional mass. We now have a *neutron star*. If white dwarfs resemble giant atoms, neutron stars are like giant nuclei with densities of a billion tons per cubic centimeter and radii that can be as small as 10 kilometers.

However, if the mass of the star is larger than 3 to 5 solar masses (recent estimates give a somewhat larger value) and the star is unable to get rid of the excess mass in one way or another, gravitational forces outweigh all other pressures. Now nothing can stop the complete collapse of the star—it will become a black hole.

Inside a Black Hole

The physical properties of a black hole are fairly simple. Like a giant—and often not-so-giant—pit, it swallows all matter that "falls" into it. The gravitational field near the edge, the horizon, is so large that it "sucks" matter from its vicinity, which then "disappears" into the hole. It makes no difference whether the collapsing matter is hydrogen, fountain pens, or rocks. All properties of the black hole are determined solely by Einstein's laws for the structure of empty space. If the hole is not rotating, its shape will be absolutely spherical. But since most stars rotate, the hole resulting from the collapse will also keep rotating. Rotation will flatten it at the poles, the same way rotation slightly flattens the Earth. It will create a swirling vortex of all matter that approaches it—like a whirlpool—and draw it into the hole. The amount of flattening and the precise shape of the hole are completely determined by the mass of the hole—which is simply related to its "radius"—and its speed of rotation. The circumference of a black hole's equator is 12 miles (19 km) multiplied by the mass of the hole and divided by the mass of the sun. Typical black holes should have masses between 5 and 50 sun's masses and circumferences between about 62 and 620 miles (100 and 1,000 km). In fact, the mass of a black hole, its speed of rotation, and its electric charge are sufficient to fix all its other properties. It is as though one could deduce every characteristic of a person from his or her weight, hair color, and eye color.

How to Identify a Black Hole

Do black holes exist? And, if so, how do we observe them? Obviously they cannot be "seen," since no light can escape from a black hole. They are too small and too far away for their gravitational fields to be noticed directly.

Suppose we have a binary star—two stars revolving around each other about a common center—in which one component is visible and the other a small "compact" star. From the motion of the ordinary star we can deduce the mass and orbital speed of its "invisible" companion. If its mass exceeds the upper limit for neutron stars (and white dwarfs), about 3 to 5 solar masses, it is very probable that we are dealing with a black hole. Indeed, such a system was observed, and the mass of the dark companion was found to be 12 to 18 solar masses, well in excess of the upper limit for neutron stars.*

If the distance between the components of a binary is small, of the same order as the star's diameter, gas will flow toward the "dark" component, raising its surface temperature. If that "star" is a neutron star or a black hole, highly energetic X rays will be emitted. As before, we differentiate between a black hole and a neutron star

*The visible star in question is Epsilon Aurigae, a star in the constellation Auriga (Charioteer), which can be seen with the naked eye.

depending on whether the mass exceeds the upper limit for neutron stars. It now appears that such a high-energy X-ray source with a sufficiently high mass has been discovered.

Looking Back

We have traveled a long and winding road. We have traced Einstein's life and work and thereby covered a lot of ground, for there is no area in physics that does not bear his imprint. His early work on the photoelectric effect—which gave quantum theory a needed "push"—and on Brownian motion—which supported the atomic theory of matter— bears witness to his youthful genius. The notion that the laws of mechanics are valid in all reference systems, the equivalence of a gravitational field with accelerated motion, and, foremost, that gravity is geometry—these are landmarks in the history of physics that will remain so forever. Einstein's later isolation from the mainstream of physics, his denial of the Copenhagen doctrine, and his unswerving pursuit of a unified field theory are the characteristics of an independent mind that dares to speculate and is not fettered by existing conventions. The motivating force of Einstein's life, from his early years in Switzerland to his last years in Princeton, was his burning curiosity to find out what makes the physical universe tick. In doing so he kept asking questions—questions that went straight to the root of the problem—and thus he obtained answers that changed our conception of space, time, and the universe as a whole.

Herblock's editorial cartoon that appeared in the Washington Post *in 1955, after the death of Einstein*

Einstein's great contributions singled him out from his contemporaries and made him, practically overnight, a world figure. He was fully aware of the adoration and esteem in which he was held, and that knowledge filled him with a graceful modesty. He did not use his fame for his own gain nor did he retreat into the "ivory tower" of his study. Rather, he raised his voice vigorously again and again against injustice and the suppression of individual liberties.

A cartoon appeared in *The Washington Post* after Einstein's death. It is a view of the universe, showing scores of planets floating by. One of these is special, for it carries a sign that reads, ALBERT EINSTEIN LIVED HERE. The world is just a little bit better because Einstein lived here.

GLOSSARY

Acceleration. Rate at which the velocity changes in the course of time. (It may be an increase or decrease in velocity, a change of direction, or both.)

Atomic theory. States that all matter is composed of atoms. An atom is the smallest particle of a chemical element that retains the chemical properties characterizing that element.

Background radiation. Extraneous signals arising from any cause that might be confused with the required measurement.

Big bang. The assumed explosive coming-into-being of the universe.

Black body. An idealized body that perfectly absorbs radiation of all wavelengths.

Black-body radiation. Electromagnetic radiation whose spectral distribution is the same as that emitted by a black body.

Black hole. A gravitationally collapsed mass (star) from which no matter, energy, or light signals can escape.

Brownian motion Small, erratic motion of light particles suspended in fluids, due to fluctuations in their collisions with surrounding molecules.

Cartesian coordinates. A system of coordinates in which the position of a point is specified by its distances from lines (or planes) at right angles to each other.

Coordinates. A set of numbers specifying the position of a point (or geometrical configuration).

Copenhagen doctrine. The generally accepted interpretation of quantum mechanics.

Doppler red shift. The change in observed wavelength of sound, radio, or light due to the motion of the source, the observer, or both. If the source is receding (moving away) the shift will be toward the red (longer wavelengths) and we speak of a *Doppler red shift.*

Electromagnetic wave. A wave produced by an accelerated or oscillating charge, which is transmitted at the speed of light.

Elementary particle. An object whose behavior and/or properties cannot be more satisfactorily described by regarding it as a compound of other particles. There are two main types of elementary particles: bosons and fermions.

Escape velocity. The minimum velocity any body must possess in the gravitational field of another body in order to escape from its gravitational attraction.

Ether. A supposed medium or substance that would act as the carrier of the electromagnetic field (light) and its energy.

Field. The description of the interaction among particles, whereby every particle is a source of the field which, emanating from the site of the source (or sources), spreads throughout space. In this picture, the force acting on a particle then results directly from the field in the vicinity and only indirectly from the sources of that field.

Frame of reference. A set of axes to which positions and motions in a system can be referred.

Frequency. Number of oscillations per unit time (such as of a wave). Its fundamental unit is the Hertz (Hz), which is one oscillation per second.

Galaxy. A large gravitationally bound collection of stellar material, containing millions to hundred billions of stars, as well as gas, dust, magnetic field, and high-energy particles.

Geodesic. The shortest distance between two points on a surface, curved or flat. Among all possible paths between two points, the geodesic is the one which takes the least time to traverse from one point to the other.

Gravitation. The mutual force of attraction that masses exert on each other.

Gravitational collapse. The sudden collapse of a massive star when the outward pressure is no longer sufficient to balance the inward gravitational pull.

Gravitational field. The field produced by masses. It acts in turn on other bodies.

Gravitational mass. The property of matter that causes it to create and be affected by a gravitational field and thus to attract and be attracted by other matter.

Gravitational red shift. A shift of the spectrum of light toward the red due to the fact that light emitted by atoms in a gravitational field is seen by a distant observer to possess longer wavelengths (than in the absence of the gravitational field).

Hubble's constant. The constant of proportionality in the relation between the recession speeds of galaxies and their distances from us.

Hubble's law. States that the distances of galaxies from us are linearly related to the red shifts (which are measures of their speeds of recession).

Inertia. That property of matter by virtue of which it persists in its state of rest or uniform motion (in a straight line, unless an external force changes that state).

Inertial frame of reference. A frame of reference with respect to which massive objects not subject to external forces move in a straight line at a uniform speed. Given one inertial frame of reference, other frames of reference moving uniformly in a straight line with respect to that frame are also inertial frames of reference.

Inertial mass. That property of matter that gives it inertia.

Inertial observer. An observer at rest in an inertial frame of reference.

Light cone. A geometric figure in four-dimensional space-time formed by the set of all directions a light signal can travel from an event (future light cone) and of all directions a light signal can travel toward an event (past light cone).

Lorentz-FitzGerald contraction. An apparent contraction along the direction of motion of objects moving at a velocity comparable to the speed of light relative to the observer.

Lorentz transformation. A transformation of coordinates in four-dimensional space-time leading from one inertial frame of reference to another.

Mass-energy relation. A relation (obtained by Einstein) giving the connection between energy and mass, according to which one can be converted into the other. Energy = mass $\times$ (velocity of light)^2.

Milky Way. The band of stars that marks the plane of *our* galaxy. Also used to denote our galaxy itself.

Neutron. An electrically neutral elementary particle with a mass of approximately that of the proton, with which it forms atomic nuclei.

Neutron star. An extremely small star with a tremendous density, whose core is composed primarily of a degenerate gas of neutrons.

Perihelion. In a planetary (elliptic) orbit about the sun, the point closest to the sun.

Photoelectric cell. Apparatus using the photoelectric effect in order to close or open electric circuits.

Photoelectric effect. The emission of electrons from special substances upon exposure to light (photons)

Photon. A "particle" that is the carrier of the electromagnetic interaction. The quantum associated with light waves.

Proton. A positively charged elementary particle (fermion) that is a constituent of atomic nuclei.

Quantum. A discrete quantity of energy; its "size" is proportional to the frequency of the wave associated with it.

Quantum mechanics. A theory developed to explain the behavior of systems of particles of the size of atoms or smaller. It differs from classical mechanics in that it gives only the probability of various measurements on the system.

Quantum theory. An extension of classical physics, needed for an adequate description of the behavior of atomic systems.

Relativity, Principle of. (restricted) If the laws of mechanics are valid in one inertial frame of reference, then they are also valid in any other inertial frame of reference. (general) All reference systems are equivalent in the description of natural phenomena, whatever may be their state of motion.

Schwarzschild radius. A critical "radius" from the center of the body within which the curvature of space is so great that neither particles nor light can escape from the body.

Tensor. A mathematical entity specified by a set of components with respect to a (given) coordinate system so that the transformation that has to be applied to these components to obtain components in another coordinate system is related to the transformation of the coordinates themselves.

Tensor calculus. A branch of mathematics that is concerned with the properties of tensors.

Time dilation. A phenomenon in special relativity due to movement near the speed of light in which the passage of time on a clock is slowed down.

Transformation. An operation by which given (mathematical) quantities are changed into corresponding ones according to definite rules.

Universe. The cosmos, all existing things, including Earth, heavens, galaxies, etc. A *closed universe* is one that is closed but without limits (like the surface of a sphere). The original expansion is insufficient to overcome the effect of gravity.

Wavelength. The distance from any point on a periodic wave to the next similar point on the succeeding (or preceding) cycle, such as crest to crest.

FOR FURTHER READING

Bergmann, Peter G. *The Riddle of Gravitation*. New York: Charles Scribner and Sons, 1968.

Bonnor, William. *The Mystery of the Expanding Universe*. New York: Macmillan, 1964.

Charon, Jean. *Cosmology*. New York: McGraw-Hill, 1970.

Clark, Ronald W. *Einstein—The Life and Times*. New York: Avon Books, 1971.

Eddington, Arthur. *The Expanding Universe*. New York: Cambridge University Press, 1958.

Einstein, Albert. *Relativity*. New York: Crown, 1961.

Frank, Philipp. *Einstein: His Life and Times*. New York: Alfred A Knopf, 1947.

Gamow, George. *Mr. Tompkins in Wonderland*. New York: Macmillan, 1944.

Hoffmann, Banesh. *Albert Einstein—Creator and Rebel*. New York: Viking Press, 1972.

Lanczos, Cornelius. *Albert Einstein and the Cosmic World Order*. New York: John Wiley & Sons, 1965.

———. *The Einstein Decade (1905–1915)*. New York: Academic Press, 1974.

Pais, Abram A. *Subtle Is the Lord*. New York: Oxford University Press, 1982.

Russell, Bertrand. *The A B C of Relativity*. New York: Harper, 1925.

Sciama, Dennis W. *The Unity of the Universe*. Winchester, Mass.: Faber, 1959.

Tauber, Gerald E. *Albert Einstein's Theory of General Relativity*. New York: Crown, 1979.

———. *Man and the Cosmos*. New York: Crown-Greenwich House, 1982.

Weinberg, Steven. *The First Three Minutes: A Modern View of the Origin of the Universe*. New York: Basic Books, 1976.

INDEX

530.11 Tauber, Gerald E.
TAU
        Relativity

$11.90   2463